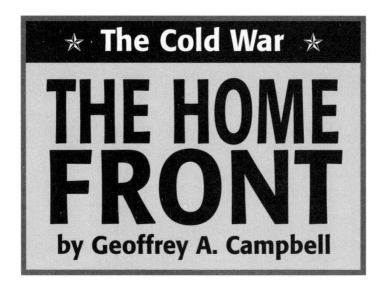

The Cold War

THE HOME FRONT

by Geoffrey A. Campbell

AMERICAN WAR LIBRARY

★★★★

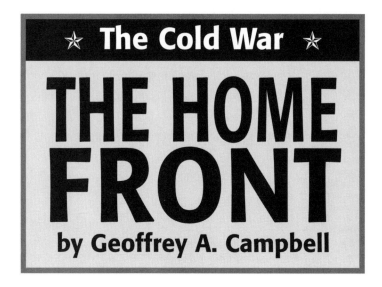

★ The Cold War ★

THE HOME FRONT

by Geoffrey A. Campbell

LUCENT BOOKS®

THOMSON

GALE

973.92
CAM

San Diego • Detroit • New York • San Francisco • Cleveland • New Haven, Conn. • Waterville, Maine • London • Munich

On cover: Children testing bomb shelter escape hatch, 1952.

To Linda, Jeff, and Larry for their steady encouragement
and support, and to all children, with the hope
they may live lives of peace.

LIBRARY OF CONGRESS CATALOGING-IN-PUBLICATION DATA

Campbell, Geoffrey A.
    The Home Front : the Cold War in the United States / by Geoffrey A. Campbell.
        p. cm. — (American war library. Cold War series)
Summary: Examines how the Cold War period in America that lasted roughly fifty
years following World War II was a contradictory time of prosperity and optimism
coupled with concerns over Soviet espionage infiltrating American institutions and
fear of nuclear apocalypse.
Includes bibliographical references (p.   ) and index.
        ISBN 1-59018-213-8 (hardback / alk. paper)
    1. United States—History—1945—Juvenile literature.   2. United States—Social
conditions—1945—Juvenile literature..   3. Cold War—Social aspects—United States—
Juvenile literature.   4. United States—Foreign relations—Soviet Union—Juvenile
literature.   5. Soviet Union—Foreign relations—United States—Juvenile literature.
[1. United States—History—1945–.   2. United States—Social conditions—1945–.
3. Cold War.   4. United States—Foreign relations—Soviet Union.   5. Soviet Union—
Foreign relations—United States.]   I. Title.   II. Series.
        E741 .C26 2003
        973.92—dc21   2002000663

Printed in the United States of America

★ Contents ★

A Nation Forged by War

The United States, like many nations, was forged and defined by war. Despite Benjamin Franklin's opinion that "There never was a good war or a bad peace," the United States owes its very existence to the War of Independence, one to which Franklin wholeheartedly subscribed. The country forged by war in 1776 was tempered and made stronger by the Civil War in the 1860s.

The Texas Revolution, the Mexican-American War, and the Spanish-American War expanded the country's borders and gave it overseas possessions. These wars made the United States a world power, but this status came with a price, as the nation became a key but reluctant player in both World War I and World War II.

Each successive war further defined the country's role on the world stage. Following World War II, U.S. foreign policy redefined itself to focus on the role of defender, not only of the freedom of its own citizens, but also of the freedom of people everywhere. During the cold war that followed World War II until the collapse of the Soviet Union, defending the world meant fighting communism. This goal, manifested in the Korean and Vietnam conflicts, proved elusive, and soured the American public on its achievability. As the United States emerged as the world's sole superpower, American foreign policy has been guided less by national interest and more on protecting international human rights. But as involvement in Somalia and Kosovo proves, this goal has been equally elusive.

As a result, the country's view of itself changed. Bolstered by victories in World Wars I and II, Americans first relished the role of protector. But, as war followed war in a seemingly endless procession, Americans began to doubt their leaders, their motives, and themselves. The Vietnam War especially caused people to question the validity of sending its young people to die in places where they were not particularly wanted and for people who did not seem especially grateful.

While the most obvious changes brought about by America's wars have been geopolitical in nature, many other aspects of society have been touched. War often does not bring about change directly, but acts instead like the catalyst in a chemical reaction, accelerating changes already in progress.

Some of these changes have been societal. The role of women in the United States had been slowly changing, but World War II put thousands into the workforce and into uniform. They might have gone back to being housewives after the war, but equality, once experienced, would not be forgotten.

Likewise, wars have accelerated technological change. The necessity for faster airplanes and a more destructive bomb led to the development of jet planes and nuclear energy. Artificial fibers developed for parachutes in the 1940s were used in the clothing of the 1950s.

Lucent Books' American War Library covers key wars in the development of the nation. Each war is covered in several volumes, to allow for more detail, context, and to provide volumes on often neglected subjects, such as the kamikazes of World War II, or weapons used in the Civil War. As with all Lucent Books, notes, annotated bibliographies, and appendixes such as glossaries give students a launching point for further research. In addition, sidebars and archival photographs enhance the text. Together, each volume in The American War Library will aid students in understanding how America's wars have shaped and changed its politics, economics, and society.

"An Iron Curtain Has Descended"

*I*t was the best of times, it was the worst of times, it was the age of wisdom, it was the age of foolishness, it was the epoch of belief, it was the epoch of incredulity, it was the season of Light, it was the season of Darkness, it was the spring of hope, it was the winter of despair, we had everything before us, we had nothing before us, we were all going direct to Heaven, we were all going direct the other way."

—Charles Dickens
A Tale of Two Cities

The Cold War years in the United States were marked by a contradiction not unlike that outlined by Charles Dickens as he began his classic *A Tale of Two Cities.* On one level, the roughly fifty-year period that marked the Cold War was one of unprecedented prosperity. The United States became a global economic leader, and Americans came to enjoy a greater material wealth than any nation in the world had ever experienced. At the same time, many Americans daily bathed in sweaty fear, believing that the United States would be subverted by the expansionist ideology of a ruthless, Communist Union of Soviet Socialist Republics (USSR) intent on conquering the United States militarily with weapons of hideous destructive force that threatened the very existence of the planet. The fact that the United States also possessed such weapons did little to provide comfort. The Cold War years in the United States can be seen as one of the most frivolous and carefree periods in the nation's history, and at the same time as one of the most serious and frightening eras. It was a time of hula hoops and pink household appliances, and simultaneously a time of espionage and possible nuclear apocalypse.

This age of both hope and despair was born of conflict between the United States and Soviet Union that arose from disagreements between the two nations following the Russian Communist revolution of 1917. Many Americans reacted with considerable alarm at the prospect of a large Soviet Union dedicated to principles that by their very terms challenged the democratic, free-market principles of the United States. Of particular concern was the Soviet Union's stated goal of establishing a new world system called communism that would, among other things, abolish private ownership in favor of government ownership and dismantle organized religion. Because of such concerns and fear that the Soviet model would influence the rest of the world, President Woodrow Wilson went so far as to send U.S. troops to the Soviet Union in 1919 in an effort to topple the government. The effort failed, and the United States did not recognize the USSR diplomatically until 1933. At that time, with the Communists firmly in control of the Soviet Union, President Franklin D. Roosevelt recognized the Communist government and established diplomatic ties between the two countries. Relations, however, remained uneasy.

The differences between the two countries were set aside when the United States and Soviet Union made common cause against Adolf Hitler and other axis powers during World War II. Many Americans looked upon their Soviet counterparts with sympathy, especially because of

Part of the Soviet Union's new world system included the Red Guards (seen below), its Communist army.

The Former Soviet Union

Arctic Ocean

Atlantic Ocean

United Soviet Socialist Republic

Europe

Asia

Pacific Ocean

Africa

Indian Ocean

the horrendous loss of life the USSR suffered at the hands of Nazi Germany. However, tensions between the two nations reemerged with a vengeance when that war was successfully concluded.

The United States emerged from the war as the strongest nation in the world. Filled with idealism, the nation wanted to share its principles of political and economic freedom throughout the world— and to see them take root and bloom. In contrast, the Soviet Union was badly battered by the war. It had lost twenty million people in the conflict. For the Soviets, national security was the primary concern. And to Soviet leaders, security meant having friendly neighbors to the nation's west. Following the war, to ensure the Soviet Union would not be invaded along its

western frontier as it had been by Hitler's Germany, the Soviets installed pro-Soviet governments in the countries of Eastern Europe. To the United States and its Western allies, the Soviet action was a direct challenge. To the Soviet Union, dominating Eastern Europe was the only policy that made sense.

On March 5, 1946, at tiny Westminster College in Fulton, Missouri, wartime British prime minister Winston Churchill addressed this conflict in one of the most memorable commencement speeches in history. As President Harry S. Truman looked on, implicitly giving his approval to the remarks by his British colleague, Churchill delivered a stinging rebuke of the Soviet occupation of Eastern Europe. He also called on all Western democracies to join in an effort to contain the spread of communism. He said:

> From Stettin in the Baltic to Trieste in the Adriatic, an iron curtain has descended across the continent. Behind that line lie all the capitals of the ancient states of central and eastern Europe. Warsaw, Berlin, Prague, Vienna, Budapest, Belgrade, Bucharest, and Sofia, all these famous cities and the populations around them lie in the Soviet sphere and all are subject, in one form or another, not only to Soviet influence but to a very high and increasing measure of control from Moscow.

> From what I have seen of our Russian friends and allies during the war, I am convinced that there is nothing they admire so much as strength, and there is nothing for which they have less respect than for military weakness. For that reason the old doctrine of a balance of power is unsound. We cannot afford, if we can help it, to work on narrow margins, offering temptations to a trial of strength. If the western democracies stand together . . . no one is likely to molest them. If, however, they become divided or falter in their duty, and if these all-important years are allowed to slip away, then indeed catastrophe may overwhelm us all.[1]

With those words the Cold War was born, and it lasted roughly fifty years. The conflict between the United States and Soviet Union was marked primarily by an escalating nuclear arms race between the two nations, spawning fears that all life on the planet could disappear if the weapons were ever used. The Cold War, however, was not all about potential military conflict or the threat of nuclear destruction. Competition between the two nations extended into the realm of economics, science, and even sports, as each nation attempted to demonstrate to the world the strengths of its respective political system. While it would be difficult to catalog the complete impact of the Cold War, one thing is clear: Life in the United States was deeply affected by its course for nearly half a century.

Chapter 1

Fear and Prosperity

On August 14, 1945, shortly after the United States dropped atomic bombs on the cities of Hiroshima and Nagasaki, President Harry S. Truman announced that Japan had surrendered, ending World War II. Victory in Europe had already been achieved with the defeat of German forces on May 8, 1945. With Truman's announcement, all fighting stopped, and euphoria swept through the United States as citizens and servicemen joined in delirious celebration. The nation's mood was best summed up in a famous photograph of a sailor and a nurse in a rapturous embrace, kissing in the midst of a giant street party in New York's Times Square. However, America's jubilation would turn in time to wary suspicion as the United States, the only nation in the world with the awful power of nuclear weaponry, became one of two major powers with "the bomb."

An American Century

As World War II came to a close, the United States enjoyed unquestioned and unparalleled world dominance. For the second time in less than thirty years, the United States had played the decisive role in ending a worldwide conflagration. At the same time, the nation had escaped the carnage and destruction that had visited Europe and Japan and enjoyed an economy in which manufacturing thrived. On February 17, 1941, prior to the United States' entrance into World War II, the publisher Henry Luce issued a call for American world leadership, claiming that if the twentieth century was "to come to life in any nobility of health and vigor, [it] must be to a significant degree an American Century."[2]

Americans appeared to have embraced Luce's call. In the years immediately following the war Europe and Japan were in a shambles. In contrast, the

A soldier and nurse in an embrace epitomized the mood of most Americans, elated by President Truman's announcement that they had won the war.

tary of the Air Force, said of the postwar period that "the United States had at least eighteen months to get ready for a war. We had the two greatest allies a country ever had in the history of the world—the Atlantic and Pacific oceans."[3] He was referring in part to America's nuclear monopoly and in part to the fact that at the time, any potential enemy would have to get across those oceans in order to attack the nation.

United States was stronger than it had been prior to the conflict. The war, and the nation's need for weapons and heavy machinery in order to fight it, had provided an unprecedented stimulus to the American economy. After the war the U.S. economy accounted for half of the world's manufacturing and nearly half of its income, boasting an unemployment rate of only 4 percent. And because of its monopoly on nuclear weapons, policy makers were able to reassure the public about the nation's security. Stuart Symington, who shortly after the war became secre-

Americans developed an overarching optimism about the future. Walter Girardin, who had left his job with Western Union to enlist in the U.S. Army, remembered returning home from the war and feeling as though he were invincible. He recalled:

In Southern California at that time, things were booming. Jobs were plentiful, and salaries were better than they were in other parts of the country. It seemed to me that everything was moving more rapidly than it had been before I left. Cities were growing, big highways were popping up everywhere, even the cars seemed faster. I felt excited by it all, and also determined to succeed and make something of myself. Suddenly I felt very confident about my future. I was assistant delivery manager for Western Union when the war broke out. When I came back, they gave me a raise of twenty-five cents more an hour, and I thought I had the world by the tail. I thought, "My gosh, I'm set for life. I've got a place to live, I can support my family, and hopefully even have more kids."[4]

Proud Americans

Evidence of U.S. superiority appeared at almost every turn. American test pilot Chuck Yeager, flying an experimental military jet, became the first man to break the sound barrier. The world's largest telescope was built at Mount Palomar in California, and the first civilian forms of powerful broad-spectrum antibiotics were developed, fueling a belief that science could conquer the scourge of disease. Engineer Presper Ecker and physicist John Mauchly at the University of Pennsylvania developed the world's first computer, called ENIAC. It took up an entire room and weighed thirty tons. Another scientific development of the same era would allow creation of handheld calculators with the same power and capacity as ENIAC; researchers at Bell

The world's first computer, ENIAC was invented by engineer Presper Ecker (right) and John Mauchly (left).

15

A Call for Leadership

Time magazine publisher Henry Luce was in many ways a visionary, seeing in the United States the potential for greatness on the world stage. On February 17, 1941, Luce wrote a lengthy essay in which he claimed that if the twentieth century were to show promise for mankind, the United States would have to take the lead. He said the United States had so far failed to undertake its leadership duty, and the result had been the beginning of World War II.

Issuing his call for an "American Century," Luce urged the United States to take a global leadership role. As reprinted in *The Ideas of Henry Luce*, edited by John K. Jessup, Luce wrote:

> In the field of national policy, the fundamental trouble with Americans has been, and is, that whereas their nation became in the 20th century the most powerful and the most vital nation in the world, nevertheless Americans were unable to accommodate

themselves spiritually and practically to that fact. Hence they have failed to play their part as a world power—a failure which has had disastrous consequences for themselves and for all mankind. And the cure is this: to accept wholeheartedly our duty and our opportunity as the most powerful and vital nation in the world and in consequence to exert upon the world the full impact of our influence, for such purposes as we see fit and by such means as we see fit.

The United States emerged from World War II as the strongest nation in the world and took the mantle of leadership Luce had urged. Many nations applauded, seeing in the United States their only hope to keep the Soviet Union from achieving its stated goal of world domination. The United States would shoulder the burden of the Cold War with the Soviet Union for nearly the rest of the twentieth century.

Laboratories invented the transistor, which in time spawned the growth of electronics.

Americans also took pride in being the only nation on earth to have harnessed the power of the atom. That pride would manifest itself in ways both large and small, including an incursion into the consumer market. The word "atomic" was used to sell a wide range of products, including such low-technology goods as sewing needles and matches. The bar at the Washington Press Club even offered an "atomic cocktail," and General Mills gave children the chance to obtain an "atomic ring" in exchange for Kix cereal box tops.

Americans were proud of their country, and that pride manifested itself in a

number of ways. Harriet Osborn, who along with her family was a pioneer living in one of the suburbs that had sprung up around American central cities following World War II, recalled the early suburban years as a celebration of America. She said:

People seemed more patriotic back then. We flew our flag on almost every holiday. If somebody had a flag of a certain size, you'd go out and buy a bigger flag. We were just keeping up with the Joneses. But regardless, we'd be flying the American colors on patriotic holidays and even on birthdays, anniversaries, and get-togethers. As I saw it, patriotism is just a love of home. In those days, we were just trying to have a good home in a good country. There were few worries. We could afford the house, and we could afford to clothe our child, and everybody else clothed their children. It was a good life. It was the American dream that we experienced, and we experienced it firsthand.[5]

It is small wonder that public service groups such as the Kiwanis International published a series of pamphlets celebrating American life, carrying such titles as "It's Fun to Live in America."[6]

Soviets Build a Bomb

The breathtaking scientific developments and the nation's burgeoning economy spurred a widespread belief among Americans that the nation's future was limitless. Evidence of that optimism manifested itself in a variety of ways, not the least of which was a phenomenal increase in the number of births. The historian William Manchester estimated that in postwar America a woman became pregnant every seven seconds. When asked about his plans at war's end, one navy officer summed up the feelings of many returning veterans when he said, "Raise babies and keep house!"[7] Men and women began to marry earlier than at any time during the century. The average age at which men married dropped to 22.8 years in 1950 from 24.3 in 1940; the average age at which women married dropped to 20.3 years in 1950 from 21.5

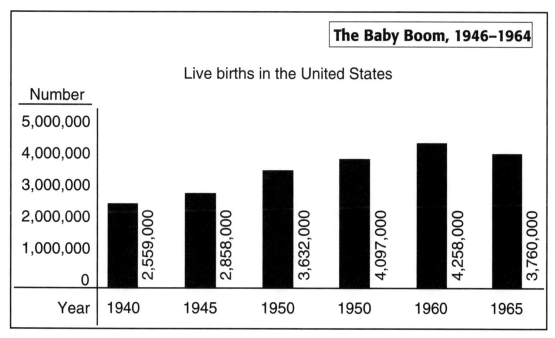

The Baby Boom, 1946–1964

Live births in the United States

Year	1940	1945	1950	1950	1960	1965
Number	2,559,000	2,858,000	3,632,000	4,097,000	4,258,000	3,760,000

in 1940. The marriage rate itself jumped from 12.1 marriages per thousand population in 1940 to 16.4 per thousand in 1946. The result is known as the baby boom. Between 1950 and 1959, 30 million American babies were born.

America's unbridled optimism, however, was relatively short lived. On September 3, 1949, an Air Force B-29 on a weather reconnaissance mission between Japan and Alaska made a staggering discovery. The plane and its crew, who were under orders to be on the alert for possible signs of nuclear testing by the Soviet Union, flew eighteen thousand feet over the Kamchatka Peninsula. Instruments on board the plane detected radiation, and filter papers on the plane, examined afterward, revealed definitive proof that the Soviet Union had tested an atomic bomb. For Americans, life would suddenly change as it became clear that the United States was no longer the world's lone superpower.

President Truman attempted to calm Americans, downplaying the discovery. In a September 23, 1949, press release announcing that the Soviets had tested a nuclear device, Truman noted that U.S. officials had long expected other nations to develop atomic bombs. He said, "Ever since atomic energy was first released by man, the eventual development of this new force by other nations was to be expected. This probability has always been taken into account by us."[8]

Truman's assurances were largely ineffective, especially when Americans learned that if the Soviets decided to drop atomic bombs on the United States, up to 15 million people could die in a single day. Nobel Prize–winning scientist Harold C. Urey, in a sentiment widely shared across America, said, "There is only one thing worse than one nation having the atomic bomb—that's two nations having it."[9]

America's optimism melted into abject fear. With the Soviet Union already spreading its influence in Europe, news of the Soviet atomic bomb fueled concern that the Soviets could now challenge the United States internationally and back up threats with nuclear might. Moreover, Americans came to see that any future war—which increasingly looked as though it would pit World War II allies, the United States and Soviet Union, against each other—would likely feature nuclear weapons and bring about the end of civilized life.

A Pervasive Fear of Attack

Americans were squeamish about the destructive power of nuclear weapons even before Truman's announcement. On August 31, 1946, the magazine *New Yorker* contained a single article, a thirty-thousand-word piece by John Hersey titled "Hiroshima." In the article Hersey dispassionately told the story of six survivors of the Hiroshima blast. Explicitly detailing the damage done by the weapons, Hersey's article focused Americans' attention on the consequences of the use of nuclear weapons. In one passage, for example, he wrote of Hiroshima victims that "their faces were wholly burned, their eye sockets were hollow, the fluid from their melted eyes had run down their cheeks."[10] The article was made into a book and was read over ABC's radio network. Hersey's work created a national furor as Americans realized that a full-scale nuclear war could lead to the extinction of the human race.

The knowledge of what atomic weapons could do, coupled with the reality that the United States was not the only nation with access to such weapons, meant that many Americans lived with a pervasive fear of a Soviet attack. Historian Ann Douglas recalled one evening in the late 1940s, when she was a child rushing from bed in fear of a Soviet invasion. She wrote that "listening to my heart beat against my pillow, I mistook it for the sound of marching feet and rushed into the living room to tell my parents, 'The Russians are coming!'"[11]

Across the United States, residents fretted about a nuclear apocalypse. Public skittishness only increased when Truman warned the nation in 1950, "I cannot tell you when or where the attack will come or that it will come at all. I can only remind you that we must be ready when it does come."[12] Truman established the Civil Defense Administration and ordered scientists to work on developing a hydro-

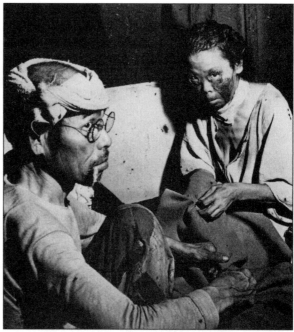

Victims of the Hiroshima atom bomb.

gen bomb. Unlike the atom bomb, which splits atoms, the hydrogen bomb gets its explosive power by fusing atoms of hydrogen, much as the sun is fueled. Truman reasoned that if the United States had a more powerful nuclear weapon, the Soviet Union would be reluctant to challenge or attack the United States. Besides, most high U.S. government officials believed the Soviets already were at work on their own hydrogen bomb. Rear Admiral Sidney W. Souers, a member of the National Security Council, told Truman, "It's either we make it or wait until the Russians drop one on us without warning."[13] Although U.S. scientists successfully tested a hydrogen device in 1952, the Soviet Union responded with a hydrogen bomb test of its own in 1953. Americans fearfully, but with renewed vigor, learned what to do in the event of a Soviet nuclear attack.

Duck and Cover

Civil defense posters urged people to "jump in any ditch or gutter . . . drop flat [and] hide your eyes in the crook of your elbow"[14] in the event of a nuclear attack. In schools across the nation children were shown civil defense films that featured Burt the Turtle, who taught them to "duck and cover," to crawl under their desks and cover their faces, should a nuclear bomb fall while they were in school. Basements in city skyscrapers were designated as fallout shelters and stocked with nonperishable food items so that nuclear-blast survivors could eat. A book sponsored by the government titled *How to Survive an Atomic Bomb* included, among other things, the suggestion that men wear hats with large brims, which readers were assured would help pro-

tect them against the heat flash of a nuclear explosion.

The Civil Defense Administration published a number of booklets offering Americans tips on surviving a nuclear attack. Carrying such titles as *Six Steps to Survival: If an Enemy Attacked Today Would You Know What to Do?*, *The Family Fallout Shelter*, and *Education for National Survival*, the booklets urged Americans to put shatterproof windows on their homes and to purchase Geiger counters, devices that measure radiation. One manual attempted to reassure Americans, claiming, "Your chances of living through an atomic attack are much better than you

Americans began building fallout shelters where families could hide to survive attack.

thought. At Nagasaki, almost 70 percent of the people a mile from the bomb lived to tell their experience."[15] The threat, however, was very real. Colorful Civil Defense Administration posters with photographs of menacing nuclear mushroom clouds grimly warned Americans that "It *can* happen Here."[16]

Americans dutifully prepared. Cities conducted air-raid drills in which citizens took shelter in the basements of buildings marked with bright yellow signs reading "FALLOUT SHELTER." In the climate of steadily growing fear of Soviet intentions, wild advice was accepted as truth. One self-proclaimed authority said dogs and cats should be shaved so that their fur would not become radioactive. Another suggested that Americans carry a drawstring bag with them at all times to pull over their heads after a nuclear blast. Entrepreneurs seriously peddled aluminum pajamas and lead-foil bras as items that could provide protection in the event of a nuclear attack. And many Americans, roughly one in every twenty, either converted their home basements into shelters or had an underground shelter built in their backyards.

A New Industry

In January 1951 Ruth Colhoun broke ground for one of the first bomb shelters to be installed in the United States and found herself besieged by reporters. The mother of three decided to spend about two thousand dollars on a shelter, and it was to be outfitted with beige concrete walls, green carpeting, and storage space for canned food. Colhoun was startled by the publicity. "It will make a wonderful place for the children to play in, and it will be a good storehouse, too. I do a lot of canning and bottling in the summer, you know."[17] A new industry was born as companies sprang up to meet the demand for bomb shelters. The Walter Kidde Nuclear Laboratories, for example, developed the Kidde Kokoon, an eight-foot by fourteen-foot steel tank. The company's three-thousand-dollar luxury model included a host of extras, including a portable three-way radio, a gasoline-powered generator, a chemical toilet, air mattresses, canned water and canned food, and protective suits that could be worn aboveground after the all clear had been sounded. For its part, A&D Bomb Shelters Inc. advertised that its shelters, built in cooperation with the nation's civil defense program, could be 100 percent financed (bought on credit).

To reinforce its message that bomb shelters were necessary, the Civil Defense Administration put together materials showing the destructive force of atom bombs. Drawn from aboveground tests conducted in Nevada, the materials showed Americans the effects of a small bomb on a house nearly a mile from ground zero. Within less than two seconds, the home was enshrouded in flames, then blasted to pieces by a shock wave before completely disintegrating.

Not only did the tests capture the nation's attention, they instilled even more fear in the already nervous public. Development of the even more destructive hydrogen bomb made survival seem very unlikely. Americans learned that if a hydrogen bomb exploded over New York City, a fireball would torch almost the entire city, and Manhattan would be split in two. Many Americans began to see nothing but futility in civil-defense efforts. The famous American writer John Steinbeck, in *Travels with Charley in Search of America*, recalled the jolt he felt outside of Minneapolis-St. Paul when he came across signs reading "Evacuation Route." "Of course, it is the planned escape route from the bomb that hasn't been dropped. Here in the middle of the Middle West an escape route, a road designed by fear. In my mind I could see it because I have seen people running away—the roads clogged to a standstill and the stampede over the cliff of our own designing."[18]

A Confident Image

The fear and uncertainty experienced by Americans was to a certain extent masked by continued outward signs of confidence and affluence. From their lives in comfortable suburban homes to their rabid pursuit of leisure activities, Americans projected an image of a people sure of their place in the world. The very rise of widespread suburban developments, which took place immediately following the war, appeared to demonstrate American ingenuity in rectifying the nation's severe housing shortage.

For example, William J. Levitt, a home builder, developed the idea of mass-produced houses. Much as Henry Ford had mass-produced affordable automobiles by developing the concept of the assembly line, Levitt figured out a way to build homes in a series of predetermined stages, allowing them to be constructed quickly and cheaply. Levitt found that there were twenty-seven steps necessary to build a home, and assigned a different team of workers to undertake each step. Although he could not build homes on a moving assembly line, as Ford did his cars, Levitt located his houses next to each other, allowing the different teams to move from one structure to another—in essence, moving the workers instead of the product they were building.

To put his dream into action, Levitt bought land on Long Island, about thirty miles outside of New York City. He then utilized his concept of teams to build identical 750-square-foot homes, creating Levittown, New York. The endeavor was a huge success—Levitt built seventeen thousand homes in his first development, selling all of them quickly at a price of under eight thousand dollars—and other entrepreneurs adopted Levitt's idea.

The American landscape soon was changed by the rise of these suburban homes. Whereas the suburbs had previously been the exclusive enclave of wealthy individuals and families, Levitt's

Located in Long Island, New York, Levittown is an example of mass-produced homes built for middle-class Americans looking for inexpensive housing in the suburbs.

concept allowed middle-class Americans to live comfortably within their means outside the bustle of the nation's cities.

"How Wonderful It Was"

Walter Girardin was one of those who snapped up new suburban tract homes. He recalled:

My wife had bought a duplex in North Hollywood while I was in the service, but it was kind of small, so I got us a VA loan and bought a bigger house down the street. Somebody had bought up an old strawberry field, divided it into lots and built forty-two

houses. They looked a little different on the outside, but they were all pretty much the same floor plan on the inside. I believe we paid $850 down for a $12,000 house, brand new. I had to work overtime to help pay for it, but oh, how wonderful it was. And there was a great camaraderie between all of the young families in the neighborhood. We used to have barbecues and parties, play golf together, and our kids ran around together. In fact when my wife was pregnant with our second daughter, I think there were ten or twelve other women in the neighborhood who were pregnant at the same time.[19]

Many critics complained the new suburbs were drab and conformist. In Levittown, for example, trees were planted in uniform twenty-eight foot intervals, and deeds even dictated the times residents could hang their wash to dry and when the lawns had to be mowed. Some critics worried that the regimentation of the suburbs was leading America into a uniform lifestyle. In his book *The Organization Man*, for example, urbanologist William H. Whyte warned that Americans

The Lure of the Open Road

Americans developed a love affair with the automobile in the postwar years that would dramatically change the nation's face. Fueled by advertising and extolled in song, many Americans thrilled at the prospect of driving new powerful cars on the open road.

Chuck Berry in a 1955 hit song perfectly encapsulated the nation's mood. As related in *As seen on TV: The Visual Culture of Everyday Life in the 1950s* by Karal Ann Marling, young people especially had an appreciation for Berry's siren song of automobile desire when he sang:

> As I was motivatin' over the hill I saw Maybellene in a [Coupe] de Ville; A Cadillac a-rollin on the open road, Nothin' will outrun my V-8 Ford.

An explosion of businesses popped up along America's roadsides, including some that later became chains and are ubiquitous today. In addition to motels such as Holiday Inn, a number of roadside restaurants promising to serve food quickly struck a responsive chord with Americans intent upon driving fast. The then-fledgling restaurants—including McDonald's and Kentucky Fried Chicken—became national icons and eventually spread throughout the world.

America's love for the automobile prompted "fast food" businesses to open along roadsides.

had given up their individuality in exchange for an opportunity to rise in the large corporations that dominated American business. Despite the criticism, however, Americans gobbled up the new homes. Levitt sold his homes almost as soon as they were finished. During the 1950s 13 million new homes were built in the United States, 11 million of them in the suburbs.

The middle class that was moving into the suburbs was growing in number, thanks to high employment rates and rising wages. Urged on by advertising, Americans clearly were attracted to what was thought of simply as "the good life."

Living in Fear and Comfort

At first glance, much of the post–World War II optimism in America might seem inconsistent with widespread fear of nuclear war. Yet some analysts have suggested America's postwar materialism was a by-product of the era's fear. Knowing that life itself could disappear in one white-hot nuclear flash from a Soviet atomic bomb, many Americans decided to live for the moment and live in comfort.

Across the nation roughly thirteen million new homes were bought between 1948 and 1958, and 83 percent of all American homes had a television set. Moreover, the number of American families with two cars doubled between 1951 and 1958. With just 6 percent of the world's population, America was consuming one-third of all the goods and services produced in the world. Nevertheless, much of America's spending spree was financed; homes and cars were purchased largely on credit, and personal debt skyrocketed. America's prosperity was uneasy, especially when viewed against the backdrop of pervasive fears that the American dream was just one Soviet bomb away from becoming an apocalyptic nightmare. Fears about nuclear annihilation similarly colored the way Americans spent their free time. Some historians see in Americans' leisure pursuits—particularly the nation's mania during the 1950s for tools, gadgets, and ready-made art kits—a search for a level of precision and certainty at a time when nuclear weapons had made life itself uncertain.

The shift to the suburbs and the increase in the number of young families in the country brought about a sea change in the nation's attitudes about work and play. Leisure time and consumerism became anthems for the nation.

Leisure and Spending

The explosion in leisure time for Americans was fueled in large measure by productivity increases that were made possible by increased mechanization and gains in efficiency. Using ever more sophisticated and precise machinery, American workers were able to produce more goods in less time than workers in previous generations. The typical American had a forty-hour work week, weekends off, and three weeks of annual vacation. Labor unions negotiated contracts that made paid holidays standard throughout the workforce. In a special report on postwar America, *Business Week* in its September 12, 1953, issue noted, "Never have so many people had so much time on their hands—with pay—as today in the United States."[20]

Americans were not simply idle, however. They spent money, and by 1954 Americans were spending about $30 billion every year on leisure activities. Many Americans spent time and money on do-it-yourself projects to enhance their otherwise drab suburban homes. Manufacturers of tools for the home-owning do-it-yourselfer discovered a growth industry as American males, especially, developed almost a cult devoted to tools and home workshops. However, purchasing the tools often ended up being an end in itself rather than a means to do actual work. Many of the men who bought the tools for home projects built little more than a workshop to house their tools. Russell Lynes, a social critic, observed, "Men love things that whirr,"[21] whether or not they are ever used for something constructive.

Many Americans turned to other hobbies, and a new market sprang up to meet their needs. Manufacturers developed kits to make model trains, model planes, stained glass, figurines, and almost anything imaginable.

Hobbies Distract Americans

By 1953 a mania for paint-by-number kits had caught on, especially among suburban housewives. The kit consisted of a canvas that was printed with outlined spaces bearing numbers that corresponded with the colors in tiny vials of oil paints. The 1950s were a time of fads, however, and even manufacturers of paint-by-number kits knew that some other craze was likely to attract the attention of consumers in time. One manufacturer said, "We pray a little, keep our fingers crossed, and hope that when the herd finally turns to glass blowing, enough will stay behind to keep us in business. In the meantime, we're cleaning up."[22] The paint-by-numbers craze proved to have some staying power as it tapped into a fundamental and strong vein in American life. Many users found the kits addictive. One woman wrote to a

Cramming

The nation was in the grips of a potential life-or-death crisis with the Soviet Union. Fears about a potential nuclear confrontation were rampant. And yet, on many college campuses the big craze was cramming—though not necessarily for exams. During the late 1950s, college students across the country engaged in a game in which they tried to squeeze as many people as possible into small spaces, such as telephone booths and Volkswagen automobiles.

The cramming craze was part of the fad-filled 1950s. Other fads included hula hoops, ducktail haircuts, and movies filmed in 3-D. The frivolity of these and other fads was in sharp contrast to the very serious tensions between the world's nuclear superpowers.

Teenagers cram into a phone booth.

Many housewives found paint-by-number kits to be addictive.

could recreate in plastic miniatures everything from trains to the battleship *Missouri*. The kits tended to be relatively easy to put together, but the details incorporated into the preformed plastic parts made them look complicated. As a result, Americans took pride in the finished product, feeling they had accomplished something meaningful when they successfully put the kits together.

paint-by-numbers manufacturer saying, "My home is disgraceful and I sit there all day and paint. I am spending money which I ought to be saving. Please send me a list of any new subjects you have."[23] Nevertheless, a backlash was in the offing as a number of other writers protested the fad, arguing that the kits stifled creativity. Still others believed paint-by-number works served as a reflection of the larger society and its regimented suburban life. One screenwriter who collected such paintings, Michael O'Donoghue, said paint-by-number paintings were "a great metaphor for life in rigid . . . America. You stayed in the lines."[24]

Model kits also became huge sellers, particularly among men. Americans

The upswing in leisure time was truly novel to postwar Americans, who had endured the deprivations and hardships of the Great Depression during the 1930s and a world war in the 1940s. Not surprisingly, Americans had a storehouse of pent-up demand, and once they had satisfied their need for food and shelter, continued their spending spree on hobbies to fill up their free time. Hobbies also served to distract Americans from the terrible reality of a possible nuclear conflagration with the Soviet Union, a conflict that held the potential to destroy all life on Earth. The fear Americans felt about a possible Soviet nuclear strike, however, would soon turn closer to home as the nation collectively began to fret about Soviet espionage in the United States.

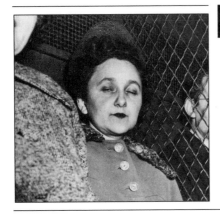

Chapter 2

The Spies Among U.S.

As Americans absorbed the awful reality of what nuclear war could mean to the world's existence, they also began to believe in and fear a broad-scale attempt by the Soviet Union to infiltrate the highest levels of the U.S. government. Highly publicized cases brought those fears to the forefront, coloring national life for years as Americans increasingly wondered whether national secrets and the security of the United States were being undermined by secret Soviet spies.

A Sense of Paranoia

Panic about Soviet spying sprang out of an atmosphere of mistrust and unease following World War II. After the Soviet Union installed pro-Soviet governments in Eastern Europe, for example, many Americans suspected the Soviet Union was positioning itself for a confrontation with the United States. Communism itself, which had attracted some interest among U.S. in-

tellectuals when the U.S. economy was devastated during the Great Depression, was viewed with increasing suspicion and hostility. A measure had even been introduced in Congress to outlaw the Communist Party. Labor unions were increasingly viewed with suspicion because of alleged Communist ties. Although he generally downplayed the threat of Soviet espionage, President Truman even decided to establish a loyalty program for federal employees, under which applicants for federal jobs could be denied employment if they had Communist ties. In addition, the FBI (Federal Bureau of Investigation) was empowered to examine the backgrounds of all federal employees to search for Communist affiliations. Employees found to have Communist ties could be removed from office. For many Americans, there was a pervasive sense of dread that the freedom and peace the nation had apparently won in World War II was slowly and inexorably being dismantled by Communist operatives throughout the world.

Against that backdrop of simmering paranoia, rumors began to circulate in Washington, D.C., that the Soviet Union had spies at the highest levels of the U.S. government. The gossip was fueled in large measure by allegations offered by several people, including a woman named Elizabeth Bentley, who claimed she had been a courier for Communist spies. Bentley took her story to the FBI in 1945 after breaking with the Communists

Elizabeth Bentley (below) claimed to have been a courier for Communist spies.

following the death of her Russian lover, spymaster Jacob Golos. Bentley's claims prompted FBI director J. Edgar Hoover to fire off a series of memoranda to Truman and Attorney General Tom Clark. However, Bentley offered no corroborating evidence, and the Truman administration let the issue lie.

In 1948 the issue of spies reached the public when Congress began to look into such allegations in an attempt to see whether the Roosevelt and Truman administrations shared blame for allowing the Communist network to thrive. Bentley was summoned before the House Un-American Activities Committee, or HUAC, to tell her story. On July 31 she testified that she had served as a go-between for Communist sympathizers in the U.S. government and Soviet agents. Bentley, who became known as the "Red Spy Queen"[25] in the press, told the committee that among her government contacts in the spy ring were prominent officials such as Harry Dexter White, who had been a senior Treasury Department official and one of the driving forces behind the creation of the World Bank before going on to become director of the International Monetary Fund. She also claimed that Lauchlin Currie, a senior assistant to President Roosevelt, was a Soviet spy, though she admitted she had never met him and had no direct knowledge of any links between Lauchlin and the Communist Party. Bentley's testimony, though explosive, was short on details, and committee members looked to find proof of Bentley's accusations.

An Ex-Communist Testifies

The panel turned to Whittaker Chambers, an admitted former Communist and spy. Prior to the conclusion of World War II, Chambers had notified a senior State Department official, Adolf Berle Jr., that the Soviets had spies throughout the State Department. However, when Berle relayed the information to President Roosevelt, the president told Berle to "go jump in the lake."[26] Now, however, the HUAC was interested in what Chambers had to say.

Like many Americans, Chambers became intrigued by communism during the 1920s because of what he saw as shortcomings in the United States' capitalist, free-market economy. Chambers said he became a Communist because "the dying world of 1925 was without faith, hope, character. Only in communism had I found any practical answer at all to the crisis, and the will to make that answer work. If it was the outrage, it was also the hope of the world."[27] However, Chambers in 1938 decided to leave the Communist Party, disillusioned by the way the Soviet Union had implemented communism and animated by a newfound belief in God, which communism prohibits. He said he came to realize that communism's triumph would mean "slavery to men wherever they fall under its sway, and spiritual night to the human mind and soul."[28] He was initially scared of Soviet reprisals and lived on the run, but then slowly reintegrated into American society. Ten years later, after a long-running stint as an editor with *Time* magazine, Chambers felt enough time had elapsed that he could go public with what he knew about Soviet espionage efforts without fear of Soviet reprisals. As Chambers put it, his decision to provide information about Soviet spying was "a simple act of war, like the shooting of an armed enemy in combat. At that moment in history, I was one of the few men on this side of the battle who could perform this service."[29]

Appearing before HUAC on August 3, the disheveled Chambers was a less than commanding witness. HUAC member and future president Richard M. Nixon recalled, "He was short and pudgy. His clothes were unpressed; his shirt collar was curled up over his jacket. He spoke in a rather bored monotone [and] seemed an indifferent if not a reluctant witness."[30] Appearances aside, however, Chambers's testimony would shake the country. Chambers himself knew that his life would never be the same. "A great public circus was being rigged, of which I was clearly to be the speaking center,"[31] Chambers later recalled of his HUAC testimony. To members of the HUAC, Chambers said:

> The publicity inseparable from such testimony has darkened, and will no doubt continue to darken, my effort

Whittaker Chambers takes the stand before the House Un-American Activities Committee (HUAC).

take] espionage."[33] He said the leader of the group was Harold Ware, the oldest son of the Communist, Ella Reeve "Mother" Bloor. Chambers said Ware found many willing converts to communism among the bright liberals who had come to Washington to staff new government programs implemented under President Roosevelt's New Deal, programs that more actively involved the federal government in the economy than ever before. By 1934 Ware had assembled a Communist network in Washington.

Chambers said the initial goal of the Ware group was to get its members into key positions in government. He said:

> The purpose of this group at that time was not primarily espionage. Its original purpose was the Communist infiltration of the American government. But espionage was certainly one of its eventual objectives. Let no one be surprised by this statement. Disloyalty is a matter of principle with every member of the Communist Party. The Communist Party exists for the specific purpose of overthrowing the Government, at the opportune time, by any and all means; and each of its members, by the fact that he is a member, is dedicated to this purpose.[34]

Chambers then dropped a bombshell. In addition to naming Harry Dexter White as a member of the Communist Party, he also implicated Alger Hiss as a

to integrate myself into the community of free men. But that is a small price to pay if my testimony helps to make Americans recognize at last that they are at grips with a secret, sinister, and enormously powerful force whose tireless purpose is their enslavement.[32]

Hiss Implicated

Chambers told the committee of a Communist group whose goal was to install Communists throughout the federal government so that they could "sway policy, make changes in personnel, or rather, influence personnel in the Government and also, if they deem[ed] fit, [under-

The Pumpkin Papers

When Whittaker Chambers decided to leave the Communist Party and stop spying for the Soviet Union, he feared that he might be assassinated to keep him from alerting U.S. officials to Soviet espionage. So worried was he about the threat of assassination, he slept with a gun. He also held on to some stolen materials and let it be widely known in the Communist underground that important spy information would be released should he meet a mysterious death. Chambers figured that if the Soviets knew he had set aside damaging information about their activities and spies in the United States, the Soviets would be less likely to kill him.

Chambers left the papers with his wife's nephew and gave them little thought until years later, when Alger Hiss filed his slander suit against him. Chambers retrieved the documents, hid them in a hollowed out pumpkin on his Maryland farm, and dropped the bombshell accusation that Hiss was not only a Communist but had also spied for the Soviet Union. Chambers led government investigators to the pumpkin, which contained rolls of microfilm that became known as the Pumpkin Papers.

Based in large part upon the Pumpkin Papers, Hiss was convicted of perjury on January 21, 1950. He nevertheless continued to protest his innocence and wrote a book in 1957 called *In the Court of Public Opinion*, in which he asserted that the Pumpkin Papers had been forged.

Later named the Pumpkin Papers, Whittaker Chambers hid Soviet documents inside hollowed out pumpkins on his property.

Communist. Hiss was a trusted and respected lawyer who had served in the federal departments of agriculture and justice prior to joining the State Department in 1936. Hiss later served as an adviser to President Roosevelt at the 1945 Yalta Conference, which also included the leaders of Great Britain and the Soviet Union, at which allied leaders planned for postwar Europe. In 1946 Hiss was elected president of the Carnegie Endowment for International Peace. Hiss's glittering resume became tarnished by Chambers, who alleged that for years Hiss had been part of the secret Communist network.

Hiss Denies Charges

A media firestorm erupted following Chambers's testimony. Papers across the country ran headlines such as "TIME EDITOR CHARGES CARNEGIE ENDOWMENT HEAD WAS SOVIET AGENT,"[35] or as the *Chicago Tribune* put it, "NEW DEAL COVERUP TOLD,"[36] a reference to the fact that neither Roosevelt nor Truman had acted when first warned that Communists had infiltrated the federal government.

Alger Hiss issued an immediate denial and demanded to be heard. In a telegram to HUAC chairman J. Parnell Thomas, Hiss said:

MY ATTENTION HAS BEEN CALLED BY REPRESENTATIVES OF THE PRESS TO STATEMENTS MADE ABOUT ME BEFORE YOUR COMMITTEE THIS MORNING BY ONE WHITTAKER CHAMBERS. I DO NOT KNOW MR. CHAMBERS AND, SO FAR AS I AM AWARE, HAVE NEVER LAID EYES ON HIM. THERE IS NO BASIS FOR THE STATEMENTS ABOUT ME MADE TO YOUR COMMITTEE. I WOULD APPRECIATE IT IF YOU WOULD MAKE THIS TELEGRAM A PART OF YOUR COMMITTEE'S RECORDS AND I WOULD FURTHER APPRECIATE THE OPPORTUNITY OF APPEARING BEFORE YOUR COMMITTEE TO MAKE THESE STATEMENTS FORMALLY AND UNDER OATH. I SHALL BE IN WASHINGTON ON THURSDAY [AUGUST 5] AND HOPE THAT THAT WILL BE A CONVENIENT TIME FROM THE COMMITTEE'S POINT OF VIEW FOR ME TO APPEAR. ALGER HISS[37]

In his appearance before the committee Hiss proceeded to draw a sharp distinction between himself and Chambers. Impeccably dressed and refined, Hiss was the physical antithesis of Chambers. He calmly and systematically refuted Chambers's charges. Hiss's emphatic denials and commanding bearing appeared to put the matter to rest, and it seemed the committee would have no choice but to drop the investigation. However, the nation's

Alger Hiss (below) testifies before the HUAC that he in fact was not a Communist.

skittishness about the allegations that Communists were in the government kept the matter alive, and newspapers continued to print articles about Chambers's accusations. Subsequent hearings also kept the issue in the news, and the nation was transfixed by the ongoing spectacle. Americans saw the case as a black-and-white issue, knowing that one of the two men was lying. In an effort to clear his name, Hiss filed slander suits against Chambers seeking seventy-five thousand dollars in damages, unintentionally opening a new chapter in the saga.

The Pumpkin Papers

Chambers responded to the suit by escalating his allegations about Hiss. Chambers claimed Hiss was not only a Communist but had been a Soviet spy as well. Chambers said Hiss had stolen sensitive State Department documents, copied them, and passed them along to Chambers so that they could be sent to Moscow. To bolster his claim, Chambers produced copies of documents he claimed Hiss had stolen from the government, and he said he had rolls of microfilm that further implicated Hiss.

Chambers had stored the microfilm in a hollowed out pumpkin at his Maryland farm. Chambers used the documents, dubbed the Pumpkin Papers, in his defense against Hiss's slander suits. The papers included longhand summaries of classified government documents, which were proven to have been written by Hiss.

Other papers included classified documents that had been copied on a typewriter later traced to Hiss. The slander cases against Chambers were dropped on the basis of the Pumpkin Papers.

Hiss's troubles were only beginning, however. He was indicted for perjury, or lying under oath, by a federal grand jury on December 15, 1948, roughly four months after Chambers's initial accusations. The indictment was for two counts of perjury. The first charge was that Hiss knowingly lied when he told Congress that he had not known Chambers; and the second was for stating that he had not "passed numerous secret, confidential, and restricted documents"[38] to the Soviets. A first trial on the charges, begun May 31, 1949, ended July 8 when the jury deadlocked, eight jurors voting to convict and four believing the government had not proven its case against Hiss.

A second trial began November 17, 1949, and this time Hiss was found guilty. On January 21, 1950, Hiss was sentenced to five years in prison. Up to his death, Hiss continued to protest his innocence. However, information subsequently made available from Soviet intelligence files clearly implicates Hiss as a Soviet spy. The significance of the Hiss case, however, far transcended issues of guilt and innocence. The case, born in an era of fear about Soviet intentions, helped to cement a broad belief among Americans that the nation's way of life was under constant Soviet attack.

Tony Hiss: "Straight to the Heart"

Tony Hiss was just seven years old when his father, Alger Hiss, was accused of having spied for the Soviet Union during the 1930s. He would spend a lifetime, however, trying to make sense of it all—and he came away convinced of his father's innocence.

In his book *The View from Alger's Window: A Son's Memoir*, Tony Hiss describes the pain and discomfort of growing up under the cloud of the allegations and conviction of his father. He wrote:

Psychologically—and paradoxically—it might have been easier to grow up thinking of Alger as guilty. At least there would have been a more familiar kind of pain to make sense of. His would have been an oft-told tale—the tragedy of a man of great promise who turns away from high purposes has been one of the towering themes of Western literature for the last twenty-five centuries: Sophocles has helped us understand such a man's inevitable humbling; Shakespeare has showed us that after this downfall all can be made right again. Such a story, for all its sadness, has a fitness to it, a rightness. If [Whittaker] Chambers's charges had been true, he, too, would be an easily recognizable figure—a scoundrel redeemed, cleansed by his repentance, a prodigal son returned home.

Had Chambers's charges been true . . . then Alger's story would today carry an abiding balm and comfort—the knowledge that it now had ended, for better or for worse, and could be laid to rest with his ashes. Because punishment is an atonement, a restitution, a public apology. Punishment balances crime; it fills in holes; it makes a vent for unbearable tensions, heals deep wounds, and lets us get on with life.

Then again—there is also punishment you don't deserve, innocence that can't make itself heard; these remain deeply disturbing, year after year. Their weight doesn't diminish; the hurts keep bleeding. They call out, but they have not been soothed or cheered, remedied or attended to—they are babies in Dumpsters and on doorsteps, refugees inching toward us on endless lines. Such situations leave their mark. Even when we hold back, hesitating to act, they pierce us straight to the heart.

Atomic Spies

The national mood darkened further when the Soviet Union tested its first atomic bomb. In September 1949, the scientific magazine *Atomics* noted,

"Though the announcement is but a few days old, the news has already rocked the nation; it is being screamed from banner headlines in every newspaper from Los Angeles to Portland, Maine, and radio commentators have worked themselves into a minor panic, many of them have the country practically at war with Russia.[39]

Such sentiments would only increase when many prominent Americans, including members of Congress, alleged that U.S. atomic secrets had been stolen by Soviet spies, hastening the development of the Soviet atom bomb. Speaking for many

Americans, Senator Karl Mundt alleged that the Roosevelt and Truman administrations had been lax in combating Soviet espionage, allowing "what were once the secrets of our atomic bomb to fall into the hands of America's only potential enemy."[40] On the other side of the Capitol, Nixon took time out from his examination of the Hiss case in September 1949 to give voice to the frustrations of many Americans over the Soviet atom bomb. "If [Truman] says the American people are entitled to know all the facts—I feel the American people are also entitled to know the facts about the espionage ring which was responsible for turning over information on the atom bomb to agents of the Russian government."[41]

Suspicions about Soviet espionage proved correct when several members of a Soviet atomic spy ring were arrested overseas. Although subsequent investigations would reveal a vast network of spies involved in stealing atom bomb secrets and getting them into the hands of the Soviet Union, much of the nation's focus was consumed by two members of the spy network, a married couple named Julius and Ethel Rosenberg. Born and raised in New York City, Julius and Ethel met each other and became friends at Communist meetings. They married in 1939 and from all appearances lived quiet, ordinary American lives. However, they were deeply committed to communism and in time became part of a larger cadre of spies that had infiltrated the nation's top secret Manhattan Project—the government's program to develop an atomic bomb.

Rosenbergs Arrested

The Rosenbergs' role in the spy ring was to receive documents pilfered by Ethel Rosenberg's brother, David Greenglass, a former machinist on the Manhattan Project. The Rosenbergs in turn passed them on to a Soviet secret agent who worked in the Soviet consulate in New York. The Rosenbergs were paid for their work and were later responsible for paying other members of the spy ring.

U.S. authorities arrested Julius Rosenberg on July 17 for his role in the spy network, and then arrested Ethel Rosenberg on August 11. The indictment against the couple alleged that the Rosenbergs were guilty of "obtaining information concerning atomic weapons, fuses, gunfire mechanisms, and other military matters"[42] with intent to pass the information to the Soviet Union. In a relatively short trial that took just fourteen days in court, the government piled up evidence of the Rosenbergs' alleged complicity in a traitorous conspiracy. The most damaging testimony against the Rosenbergs came from Ethel's brother, Greenglass, who described in detail the sorts of atomic secrets he had provided to the Rosenbergs.

Despite the array of evidence presented against them, the Rosenbergs issued staunch denials. Although they were Communists, the Rosenbergs repeatedly invoked their right under the U.S. Consti-

Julius and Ethel Rosenberg were found guilty of obtaining secret U.S. military information with intent of passing it to the Soviets.

April 5, 1951, Judge Irving Kaufman announced his sentence to a rapt nation. Kaufman noted that a Soviet citizen accused of treason in the USSR would have been summarily executed without even the charade of a trial, saying he believed the trial accorded to the Rosenbergs reflected the true values of the United States. According to Kaufman, those values were under attack because of people like Julius and Ethel Rosenberg. He said:

> It is so difficult to make people realize that this country is engaged in a life and death struggle with a completely different system. This struggle is not only manifested externally between these two forces but this case indicates quite clearly that it also involves the employment by the enemy of secret as well as overt outspoken forces among our own people.[43]

tution's Fifth Amendment not to answer direct questions about their Communist affiliations. They reasoned that simply by admitting to being Communists, they would invite the jury to find them guilty of spying for the Soviets. Their refusal to answer, however, had the same effect. Coupled with their denials of any involvement in spying for the Soviets, their refusal to answer questions about their politics left an impression in many minds that they were, in fact, guilty.

Rosenbergs Found Guilty

The jury reached that conclusion on March 29, 1951, finding that Julius and Ethel Rosenberg were guilty of conspiring to spy against the United States. On

Judge Kaufman said the Rosenbergs had by their actions made clear where their allegiances lay, and he offered his personal feelings about the nuclear theft:

> I consider your crime worse than murder. Plain deliberate contemplated

murder is dwarfed in magnitude by comparison with the crime you have committed. In committing the act of murder, the criminal kills only his victim. The immediate family is brought to grief and when justice is meted out the chapter is closed. But in your case, I believe your conduct in putting into the hands of the Russians the A-bomb years before our best scientists predicted Russia would perfect the bomb has already caused, in my opinion, the Communist aggression in Korea, with the resultant casualties exceeding fifty thousand and who knows but that millions more of innocent people may pay the price of your treason.[44]

Kaufman was referring to the Korean War, implying that the Soviet-backed North Koreans would not have gone on the offensive had the Soviet Union not had atomic weapons at its disposal.

Kaufman went on to say that any punishment for the Rosenbergs must send a clear signal to the world that the United States would not tolerate treason, "that this nation's security must remain inviolate; that traffic in military secrets, whether promoted by slavish devotion to a foreign ideology or by a desire for monetary gains must cease."[45]

Barely concealing his contempt for the Rosenbergs, Kaufman added:

What I am about to say is not easy for me. I have deliberated for hours, days

The Rosenberg Files

Although Julius Rosenberg protested his innocence against charges that he stole atomic bomb secrets for the Soviet Union, once-secret Soviet files recently made available to researchers demonstrate that Rosenberg was a dedicated Soviet operative. His Soviet handlers viewed him with an almost fatherly affection, and were deeply concerned that his activities on their behalf not be discovered by U.S. authorities.

One memo about Rosenberg contained in the Soviet files was written shortly after Rosenberg was fired from a job when his membership in the Communist Party was discovered. The memo, as reprinted in *The Haunted Wood: Soviet Espionage in America—the Stalin Era*, by Allen Weinstein and Alexander Vassiliev, noted that in Rosenberg

> we have a man devoted to us, whom we can trust completely, a man who by his practical activities for several years has shown how strong is his desire to help our country. Besides, in [Rosenberg] we have a capable agent who knows how to work with people and has solid experience in recruiting new agents. . . .

> In our current relations with him, it must be explained that his fate is far from indifferent to us, that we value him as a worker, and that he, undoubtedly, may and must rely on assistance from outside.

and nights. I have carefully weighed the evidence. Every nerve, every fiber of my body has been taxed. I am just as human as are the people who have given me the power to impose sentence. I am convinced beyond any doubt of your guilt. I have searched the records—I have searched my conscience—to find some reason for mercy—for it is only human to be merciful and it is natural to try to spare lives. I am convinced, however, that I would violate the solemn and sacred trust that the people of this land have placed in my hands were I to show leniency to the defendants Rosenberg.

It is not in my power, Julius and Ethel Rosenberg, to forgive you. Only the Lord can find mercy for what you have done.

The sentence of the Court . . . is, for the crime for which you have been convicted, you are hereby sentenced to the punishment of death, and it is ordered . . . you shall be executed according to law.[46]

Death Sentence Divides Country

The Rosenbergs launched a number of legal appeals to overturn their death sentence, and their supporters also appealed to the public for mercy. Among those who protested the death sentence for

The death sentence placed on the Rosenbergs prompted many protests from the public.

the Rosenbergs were a number of non-Communists worldwide who thought the Rosenbergs were guilty but nevertheless abhored the idea of killing the parents of two young sons. Even the Roman Catholic pope urged clemency (mercy) for the couple. In major cities throughout the United States, thousands of demonstrators either claimed that the Rosenbergs were innocent or that their sentence was too harsh. They noted that Greenglass, for example, had received a sentence of only fifteen years in prison, and he had admitted that he stole atomic secrets. Members of the clergy, some scientists, political liberals, and others joined forces on behalf of the Rosenbergs. A number of petitions were made to President Dwight D. Eisenhower to spare the Rosenbergs their lives. Americans, however, were clearly polarized. Equally large crowds demonstrated in favor of the Rosenbergs' execution, carrying signs with messages such as "Kill the Dirty Spies."[47]

After the Rosenbergs' final legal appeal was denied by the U.S. Supreme Court on June 19, 1953, President Eisenhower rejected a last-ditch petition for clemency. He reasoned, "I can only say that by immeasurably increasing the chance of atomic war, the Rosenbergs may have condemned to death tens of millions of innocent people over the world."[48] The Rosenbergs were executed in the electric chair at Sing Sing prison in Ossining, New York, that evening. Julius was put to death at 8:06 P.M., and Ethel at 8:15 P.M. Protesters on both sides of the Rosenberg saga stood vigil outside the White House in Washington. While pro-Rosenberg forces prayed quietly, anti-Rosenberg protesters noisily celebrated the executions and waved signs with such tasteless messages as "Two Fried Rosenbergers Coming Right Up."[49]

The Hiss and Rosenberg trials took place in the context of a growing national apprehension that a world the United States had seemed to rule only years earlier was suddenly under constant Communist attack. That apprehension translated itself into a fear and hatred of anything that could be construed as un-American. The trials themselves became symbols of an age of fear and helped to set the stage for one of the darkest periods in American history—a nationwide witch-hunt for Communists in which lives and livelihoods could be destroyed by mere accusations.

Chapter 3

McCarthyism

The furor surrounding the Hiss and Rosenberg scandals created a national environment of dread that the highest levels of the United States government had been infiltrated by operatives of the Soviet Union. Moreover, communism itself appeared to be ascendant across the globe as China became Communist after a bloody civil war and Soviet-backed Communist troops were battling for control of Korea. Many Americans lived in a state of anxiety, frightened that the United States itself could become the next battleground. The nation's angst only increased when Republican Senator Joseph McCarthy of Wisconsin charged that the government had become honeycombed with Communists who were plotting the overthrow of America's democratic way of life.

A Fateful Speech

As 1950 dawned, Senator McCarthy was relatively unknown outside Wisconsin.

His career, and the nation's history, took a sudden turn on February 9, 1950, however, when McCarthy appeared before the Women's Republican Club of Wheeling, West Virginia. McCarthy arrived in Wheeling with two speeches, one on housing and the other on the issue of Communists in government. McCarthy was indifferent to which speech he delivered and asked the local Republican who picked him up at the airport to choose. Urged to use the Communist speech, McCarthy quickly warmed to the task.

In the speech he warned that the United States was besieged by Communist forces. As McCarthy put it that day, "I have here in my hand a list of 205 names known to the secretary of state as being members of the Communist Party and who nevertheless are still working and shaping the policy of the State Department."[50]

When reporters later asked McCarthy for a copy of the speech, McCarthy claimed to have lost it. However, he recreated it and had it inserted into the *Congressional Record*, the official record of congressional proceedings. In this version McCarthy revised the number of alleged Communists in the State Department to fifty-seven. In neither case, however, did McCarthy have any proof of the allegations. Nevertheless, journalists swept up in the general hysteria about communism unquestioningly reported McCarthy's claims. Emboldened by the publicity and generally favorable response from Americans, McCarthy continued his crusade.

Senator Joseph McCarthy accused many in the State Department of being Communist.

"Twenty Years of Treason"

McCarthy proceeded to go on a relentless rampage, holding court for the next four years as the nation's chief inquisitor. In a reckless style that soon earned the name "McCarthyism," the senator lobbed unsubstantiated charges at respected figures, never offering any evidence. In time, merely being accused by McCarthy was tantamount to a guilty verdict in the eyes of many Americans. That was true even though McCarthy never actually proved that anyone in government was a Communist, and being a Communist was neither a crime nor a bar to government employment.

McCarthy's favorite targets were Democrats, whom he likened to a front for Communists. He claimed Democrats were guilty of "20 years of treason"[51] in part, he said, because the Democratic administrations of Roosevelt and Truman had not acted to root out the supposed hordes of Communists in government. Anyone, however, could become a potential target of McCarthy's smear campaign. He alleged that Owen Lattimore, a State Department expert on Mongolia, was "the top Russian spy."[52] He even attacked the revered George C. Marshall, a highly respected World War II general who was the driving force behind the Marshall

Plan, which rebuilt Europe in the aftermath of World War II. But according to McCarthy, Marshall was "an instrument of the Soviet conspiracy"[53] that, he said, amounted to "an infamy so black as to dwarf any previous such venture in the history of man."[54]

McCarthy did not tolerate anyone who was not enthusiastically behind his campaign, asserting that anyone who was against him was for the Communists. When some of McCarthy's Senate colleagues called his bluff on the charges he made in his Wheeling speech, labeling the allegations fraudulent in a motion approved by a Senate subcommittee, McCarthy promptly retaliated. He organized a team to go into Maryland to smear the subcommittee's chairman, Senator Millard Tydings of Maryland. McCarthy's group produced a doctored photo purporting to show Tydings talking amiably with a known senior American Communist. In truth, the men had never had a conversation. McCarthy's group had simply taken a photo of Tydings and pasted a picture of the Communist on it, then rephotographed it. The picture appeared in a campaign tabloid and helped doom Tydings's Senate career as many Maryland voters were deceived by the fake.

McCarthy Scares Opponents

As a politician, McCarthy proved himself a master. Correctly measuring the nation's mood in the wake of the Hiss and Rosenberg espionage cases, McCarthy rode a crest of newfound celebrity simply by claiming to find Communists throughout government. Many Americans applauded his efforts as courageous and patriotic. Many other Americans quietly watched, afraid to raise their voices in protest. These silent detractors were scared off by the Tydings incident and the certain knowledge that they, too, could be labeled as Communists. Not even the president of the United States felt strong enough to battle McCarthy when the senator was at the height of his powers. President Dwight D. Eisenhower, for example, loathed McCarthy but refused to challenge him, claiming that saying anything would merely provide McCarthy with more ammunition. Eisenhower said, "I just will not—I refuse—to get down into the gutter with that guy."[55] Privately, however, Eisenhower felt he might be vulnerable to McCarthy's smears, because some of his wartime decisions as a general in the army had unintentionally but ultimately allowed the Soviet Union to gain control of Eastern European nations.

McCarthy's relentless anti-Communist campaign drew widespread public support. Many Americans were pleased that finally someone in the government was doing something to ferret out Communists, not realizing that McCarthy's claims of Communist infiltration were fictional. A May 21, 1950, Gallup poll revealed that 84 percent of Americans were aware of McCarthy's campaign, and 39 percent

Senator McCarthy enjoyed public support during the 1950s, as it was widely believed that he was doing the United States a great service.

believed that what he was doing was beneficial to the nation. Only 29 percent believed McCarthy's charges were hurting the country, with 16 percent reporting that they had no opinion on the matter. By the beginning of 1954 Gallup pollsters found that a strong 50 percent of Americans were supportive of McCarthy's crusade against communism.

McCarthy ushered in a period of rampant and often misguided hysteria. His fantastic charges fanned the flames of people's ugliest instincts and fears, and average Americans came to confuse polit-

ical liberalism with communism. Moreover, Americans went out of their way to avoid looking as though they agreed with, or condoned, any aspect of communism. For example, some schools banned performances of "Robin Hood" because of its alleged Communist themes (that of taking from the rich and giving to the poor). In Wheeling, West Virginia, the city manager complained about some prizes in chewing gum packages. The prizes, cards that represented the world's nations, included one that said, "USSR popn. 211,000,000, Capital Moscow."[56] The city manager complained, "That's a terrible thing to expose children in this city to."[57] Newspaper readers howled in protest and anger when, after the Cincinnati Reds defeated the New York Yankees in an exhibition baseball game, newspaper reports of the contest were headlined, "Reds beat Yanks."[58] The Reds themselves began to go by the name of "Redlegs" to avoid the appearance of any endorsement of Communists, who were called "Reds" because of the color of their flag. Not to be outdone, the city council of Moscow, Idaho, sought to insulate itself from any negative commentary when it passed a resolution that read, "Whereas the citizens of Moscow, Idaho, believe they have a prior and superior title to the name . . . Moscow, USSR [should] change [its capital's name] from Moscow to some name that will not by association embarrass the citizens of Moscow, USA."[59]

McCarthyism Pervades American Life

McCarthyism also had broader implications for Americans. The historian Harold Evans has noted that McCarthy's

> unscrupulous, swaggering genius paralyzed the Truman administration,

cowed President Eisenhower, mesmerized most of the press, lethally warped foreign policy for a decade, frightened academia, turned friend against friend, wrecked countless careers and moved millions to suspicion of fellow citizens guilty of nothing more than perhaps a subscription to a leftist publication or the courage to stand up to the demagogue.[60]

Although his stated goal was to protect the United States from alleged Communist subversion, McCarthy unwittingly made the nation more like the USSR than the senator ever acknowledged. Several of McCarthy's Senate colleagues, however, clearly saw where McCarthy was taking the country and were worried enough to sign a "Declaration of Conscience" decrying McCarthy's techniques. In a Senate speech on June 1, 1950, Senator Margaret Chase Smith of Maine noted, "The United States Senate has long enjoyed worldwide respect as the greatest deliberative body in the world. But recently that deliberative character has too often been debased to the level of a forum of hate and character assassination sheltered by the shield of congressional immunity."[61] Senator Smith quoted from the declaration, asserting, "It is high time that we all stopped being tools and victims of totalitarian techniques—techniques that, if continued here unchecked, will surely end what we have come to cherish as the American way of life."[62] However, most lawmakers remained afraid of Senator McCarthy's power and influence.

McCarthy's campaign had a chilling effect on free speech, as many Americans found themselves afraid to speak out on issues of national importance. Those who did find the courage to speak often found themselves arrested or their careers ruined—especially black Americans. For example, W.E.B. DuBois, an African American intellectual and outspoken voice in the nation's civil rights movement, was arrested in 1950. His crime was nothing more than membership in a group that worked for world peace, including peace between the United States and Soviet Union. Likewise, African American actor Paul Robeson lost his passport and found his career in a shambles after he forcefully spoke out in favor of black equality. Civil rights leader Martin Luther King Jr. was targeted by the FBI because some in government believed that King's challenge of segregation in the South and his call for equal rights were Communist inspired. Senator McCarthy and his allegations created a national environment of distrust, and neighbors and coworkers cast a wary eye on each other, looking for evidence of possible Communist ties.

High Noon in America

McCarthyism's impact spread to every aspect of American society, including the entertainment industry. Many movie stu-

The Civil Rights Struggle

The influence exerted by the Cold War extended throughout American society. In addition to shaping popular attitudes about communism and the need to develop a nuclear arsenal, Cold War sensibilities also helped create a climate in which civil rights for African Americans finally assumed a prominent place in the national agenda.

As blacks and sympathetic whites across America, especially in the nation's South, challenged legal segregation that largely separated blacks and whites, government officials fretted about how the lawsuits, boycotts, and demonstrations would appear to people in other countries. They worried that the nation's unfair treatment of blacks would hurt the United States in its bid to enlist support against the Soviet Union. They understood that the United States, which purportedly stood for freedom and equality in contrast to the unrelenting governmental control inherent in Soviet communism, might lose influence with nations around the globe unless steps were taken to eliminate segregation.

The government began to take active steps to remove segregative practices from American life. The government even sent troops to enforce Supreme Court rulings that integrated public schools. However, change would come slowly and only with the courage and strength of committed blacks and whites who often put their own lives in jeopardy in order to break down centuries-old prejudices.

dios shied away from controversial subjects, and bland musicals became common movie fare. There were exceptions, however. For example, Arthur Miller's 1952 play *The Crucible* was widely viewed as a protest about rampant McCarthyism. Ostensibly about the 1692 Salem witch trials, in which a number of women were accused of being witches and sentenced to death, Miller's play had clear parallels with McCarthy's anti-Communist crusade. In addition, a popular 1952 western called *High Noon* told the story of a sheriff who alone had the courage to stand up to outlaws. Although the sheriff knew his life would be easier if he simply ran away, he believed that the town would never be safe if someone did not resist the outlaws. The movie, which starred Gary Cooper and Grace Kelly, was seen by a number of Americans as a call to resist McCarthyism.

The truth and public opinion began to catch up to McCarthy when in April 1954 he launched an investigation of the U.S. Army for alleged subversion. The investigation was triggered when McCarthy assistant David Schine was drafted by the army. McCarthy's chief counsel, Roy Cohn, was particularly fond of Schine and convinced McCarthy to fight the army.

When the army refused McCarthy's request that Schine be given a commission and allowed to forgo boot camp, a physically and mentally grueling period of basic training, McCarthy retaliated with a blistering—and entirely fabricated—crusade. He accused the army of harboring known Communists and claimed to have uncovered a spy ring at the Army Signal Corps at Fort Monmouth, New Jersey.

McCarthy Versus the Army

The grudge match between McCarthy and the army would reach new lows, however, after the army informed Cohn that Schine was likely to receive an overseas posting. Cohn threatened to smear Army Secretary Robert T. Stevens, prompting Defense Secretary Charles Wilson to warn McCarthy that unless Cohn were fired, the army would release a fully detailed account of

Senator McCarthy claimed that controversial photos taken of his assistant had been altered.

Cohn's ill-advised efforts on Schine's behalf. McCarthy refused and retaliated by fabricating documents that he said showed that the army had used Schine as a means of stopping McCarthy's investigation of the army. McCarthy's colleagues, fed up with the senator's tactics, voted to launch a full inquiry into McCarthy's feud with the army.

The so-called Army-McCarthy hearings were televised, and many Americans for the first time saw McCarthy in action. As 80 million Americans watched the hearings unfold over thirty-six days, many viewers came away disillusioned by McCarthy's mean-spirited attacks. Still more were troubled by McCarthy's fabrication of evidence and his disregard for the facts. Almost all viewers were transfixed by the army's lawyer, Joseph Welch of Hale & Dorr, who consistently outmaneuvered McCarthy and Cohn in a calm, measured tone. The culmination of McCarthy's downfall came when the senator, ignoring a previous agreement with Welch, smeared a young lawyer on Welch's staff with accusations of a previous Communist affiliation.

Welch quietly but firmly rebuked McCarthy, asserting that he had no idea McCarthy "could be so reckless and so cruel as to do an injury to that lad."[63] Welch added, "I like to think I am a gentleman, but your forgiveness will have to come from someone other than me."[64] Welch then concluded, to an outburst of applause from a rapt audience, "Let us not assassinate this lad further, Senator. You have done enough. Have you no sense of decency, sir, at long last? Have you left no sense of decency?"[65]

Following the showdown, polls showed that only 34 percent of Americans continued to support McCarthy. Senators who had long feared McCarthy finally felt emboldened to take a stand against the Wisconsin senator's heavy-handed ways. A Senate committee recommended that McCarthy be censured for his conduct. However, McCarthy was not yet through with his reckless allegations. He characterized the committee that recommended his censure as the "unwitting handmaiden" of the Communist Party[66] and charged that, when writing its report, the committee "imitated Communist methods—that it distorted, misrepresented, and omitted in its effort to manufacture a plausible rationalization."[67] McCarthy had finally gone too far, and the Senate on December 2, 1954, voted to censure McCarthy, a largely symbolic action that in effect told the nation that members of the Senate wished to distance themselves from McCarthy and repudiate his actions. In practice, however, the condemnation had greater meaning. By publicly denouncing him, the Senate effectively stripped McCarthy of legitimacy, ending his reign of terror under the auspices of the U.S. Senate.

Suspicions About Labor Unions

Although McCarthy has subsequently become a leading symbol of one of the darkest periods in American history, it is far from clear whether someone else might not have launched an identical crusade. Indeed, many government investigations that are lumped under the category of McCarthyism actually predated the senator's hunt for Communists. For example, many Americans had by the 1940s grown concerned about the possible Communist infiltration of labor unions. In a 1944 memorandum, FBI director J. Edgar Hoover warned, "The Communists will only be a menace to U.S. if they can seize labor control & this they are gradually doing."[68] By 1946 the FBI had concluded that Communists "unquestionably would sabotage this country's effort in resisting Russia and that this . . . is a great and

The Father of the A-bomb Loses His Security Clearance

J. Robert Oppenheimer helped usher in the atomic age as head of the nation's Manhattan Project, but the experience left him so shaken he wanted no part in developing an even more powerful hydrogen bomb. Although he was joined by many in the scientific community in his opposition to development of the so-called Super bomb, his position would later cost him politically.

In a later security hearing, held in 1953, an array of people who had successfully pushed for creation of a hydrogen bomb and those who felt slighted by Oppenheimer in the past thought they saw an opportunity for revenge. They trotted out well-worn rumors about Oppenheimer's alleged associations with Communists—his wife, Kitty, and brother, Frank, were both Communists—and introduced what they said was evidence that Oppenheimer was linked to a Soviet espionage ring. Nevertheless, forty well-respected people in government and scientific circles testified on Oppenheimer's behalf.

Although the panel conducting the hearing rejected claims that Oppenheimer was a spy, it nevertheless refused to continue his security clearance, which meant that one of the nation's top scientists would no longer be able to work on sensitive projects.

Dr. J. Robert Oppenheimer refused to assist in the further development of hydrogen bombs. As a result supporters of the bomb persecuted Oppenheimer as being a Communist spy.

total danger to the security of this Nation."[69] That same year Clark Clifford, an aide to President Truman, was more pointed. He argued that Communists would attempt to strengthen their hold over unions. He said, "This would cripple the industrial potential of the United States by calling strikes at those times and places which would be advantageous to the Soviet Union."[70]

Fueling such concerns was knowledge that Communists had already pulled strikes against U.S. defense interests. In 1940 and 1941, for example, the Communist Party in the United States had pursued an ardent antiwar program. During that time, Communist-led unions at U.S. defense plants staged strikes, bolstering fears that Communists could use labor to disrupt U.S. industry. A string of strikes following World War II led Truman in exasperation to note, "The Reds, the phonies and the 'parlor pinks' seem to have banded together and are becoming a national danger. I am afraid that they are a sabotage front for Uncle Joe Stalin."[71]

Concerns about the potential for Communist sabotage reached such a level that Congress began investigating the issue in 1947. After hearings before both the House and Senate labor committees, Congress approved the Taft-Hartley Act, which set limits on union activities. Among other things, the law prohibited unions from forcing employees to become union members. The law also required union officials to sign affidavits declaring that they were not Communists.

The Allis-Chalmers Strikes

The idea behind the Taft-Hartley Act was to limit the power of the unions in case they were infiltrated by Communists. Of particular concern were strikes in 1941 and 1946 at the Milwaukee Allis-Chalmers Manufacturing Company, which was involved in defense production, including work on the Manhattan Project. Louis Budenz, a former Communist and editor of the Communist *Daily Worker* testified before HUAC that the two strikes at Allis-Chalmers had been ordered by the American Communist Party (his allegations would lead to a perjury conviction against Local 248 president Harold Christoffel). Although many scholars now believe that Budenz's charges were fabricated, at the time they were considered proof that domestic Communists were as large a threat to the United States as those in the Soviet Union. Even the U.S. Supreme Court referenced the Allis-Chalmers strikes as evidence of a Communist threat to domestic security and defended Congress' right to require union officials to sign affidavits that they are not Communists. Chief Justice Fred Vinson said the Taft-Hartley Act did not violate the free speech guarantee of the Constitution's First Amendment, adding that the affidavit requirement "is designed to protect the public not against what Communists and others identified therein advocate or believe, but against what Congress has concluded they have done and are likely to do again."[72] Much as the Hiss and Rosenberg cases would become emblematic of the threat of espionage, the Allis-Chalmers strikes became symbolic of a perceived Communist threat of industrial sabotage.

Labor unions were not the only group to attract congressional scrutiny; lawmakers soon turned their attention to the nation's entertainment industry. In 1947 HUAC launched an investigation of the motion picture industry on the grounds that Communist leanings among Hollywood figures could color their work and thereby influence American viewers. According to some committee members, movies held great sway with the American people and could therefore corrupt society and disrupt the nation's stability. In the HUAC's view, any movie that was sympathetic to Communism could undermine the country.

The resulting hearings were often marked by impassioned and angry exchanges as lawmakers asked Hollywood figures the question, "Are you now or have you ever been a member of the Communist Party?"[73] A number of prominent actors, including Humphrey Bogart and Lauren Bacall, traveled to Washington to protest the hearings, and soon found themselves the target of congressional wrath. Bogart, for example, felt threatened enough to take out advertisements asserting that he was not a Communist. "Hell, I'm no politician. . . . [O]ur

Humphrey Bogart (center), Lauren Bacall (right), as well as many other actors traveled to Washington, D.C. to protest Congress' investigation into Communist activity in Hollywood.

The Hollywood Blacklist

Rampant McCarthyism touched nearly every facet of American life. One particularly hard-hit sector was the entertainment industry, where actors were blacklisted if there was even the slightest suspicion of Communist sympathy.

Actress Lee Grant made the blacklist because she found it unfair that some of her colleagues were being browbeaten by the House Un-American Activities Committee. It was far from an exclusive club. As Grant related to Peter Jennings and Todd Brewster in *The Century*:

There really weren't very many Communists in Hollywood. And they were not a paramilitary group—they were writers and composers and actors posing no real threat to anyone. But once the anti-Communists had taken care of the real Communists, they started picking on people who had given money to certain organizations, people who had shown up at the "wrong" party, or people who voted for the "wrong" person—people who weren't even political at all, like me. And the entertainment industry buckled under the pressure. A grocer in Syracuse, for example, ran a successful campaign against actors. He filled his supermarkets with signs that said things like, "If you buy Colgate Toothpaste you are buying a product that sponsors this program with this actor, who is a Communist." And when people started contacting the networks about it they would just take those actors right off the programs.

Washington trip was a mistake,"[74] he said in explaining the advertisements.

HUAC would call a total of nineteen Hollywood actors, directors, and writers to testify. Ten refused to answer when questioned about whether they were or had ever been Communists. One Hollywood figure, Ring Lardner Jr., was badgered mercilessly when he refused to answer. In exasperation, Lardner finally told the committee, "I could answer . . . but if I did I would hate myself in the morning"[75] because he found the entire proceeding un-American.

The Hollywood Blacklist

Known as the Hollywood Ten, those who refused to testify before Congress were held in contempt and served sentences of up to one year in prison. Hollywood executives quickly moved to insulate their industry from charges that it was harboring Communists. The Association of Motion Picture Producers issued a statement disassociating itself from Communists and pledged to be vigilant in keeping Communists from working in Hollywood. The statement by the producers said, "We will not knowingly employ a Communist nor a member of any party or groups which advocates the overthrow of the Government of the United States by force or by illegal or unconstitutional methods. . . . [W]e will invite the Hollywod talent guilds to work with us to eliminate any subversives, to protect the innocent, and to safeguard free speech and a free screen wherever threatened."[76] The entertainment "blacklist" was thus born, and hundreds of actors, singers, writers, and others would subsequently find it hard to get work. Among those singled out for exclusion were composer and conductor Leonard Bernstein; actors Lee J. Cobb, Jose Ferrer, and Will Greer; writer Dashiell Hammet; and actor-director Orson Welles.

As the congressional investigations into labor and entertainment demonstrate, Senator Joseph McCarthy was as much a symptom of the nation's paranoia about Communists as he was its cause. This dark period in American history will forever be known for its rampant McCarthyism, even though many of its signature events and investigations long predated the arrival of the Wisconsin senator. As events throughout the world seemed to overtake the nation, Americans became edgy and concerned about Communist intentions in the United States. The national reaction to the perceived threat, however, seriously damaged the nation's long-standing commitment to free expression and thus made the United States more like the Soviet Union than McCarthy would ever admit.

Chapter 4

The Space Race

Americans emerged from the McCarthy era with a newfound sense of confidence and enthusiasm. This new attitude took root in part because scientific advances in the United States appeared poised to turn science fiction into reality as the nation prepared to launch the world into the long-held dream of space exploration. In time, however, Americans would discover that the Soviet Union was also committed to exploring outer space. A great contest ensued, pitting the two superpowers against each other in a race to be the world's first to launch humans beyond the pull of Earth's gravity.

United States Banks on a Space First

The United States had announced that it would send a satellite into Earth orbit as part of its contribution to the International Geophysical Year, a global, eighteen-month effort that stretched from July 1957 to the end of 1958. The program was designed to find out as much as possible about the earth, sun, and outer space, and Americans believed the United States' contribution to the project would demonstrate the nation's technological superiority. The Soviet Union also said it would launch a satellite, but the announcement was largely ignored in the West as attention focused on the U.S. Navy's *Vanguard* satellite, which was scheduled for a November 1957 launch.

By the middle of 1957 bookstore shelves were filled with books about the *Vanguard*, and popular magazines regularly heralded the impending American scientific achievement. As early as 1956 Americans had no doubt the United States would be the first into space. In its February 1956 issue, *National Geographic* magazine detailed the upcoming *Vanguard* triumph as "history's first artificial earth-circling satellite."[77] A month later the magazine trumpeted *Vanguard* as the "first true space vehicle."[78] Across the nation, scientists spoke to rapt audiences about the upcoming triumph, and the very notion of satellites had become fixed in the national consciousness as symbolic of good old American know-how.

Nevertheless, the *Vanguard* project was suffering from problems. The satellite itself was ready to go, but scientists were having trouble with the rockets necessary to boost the satellite into orbit. The three stages of rockets needed to achieve orbit were proving problematic. The first stage was not powerful enough, the second required a redesign, and the third weighed too much. The planned 1957 launch was pushed back to early 1958. Nevertheless, Americans accepted it as an article of faith that the United States would beat the Russians into space. The Soviet Union, most Americans believed, was hopelessly backward in technology, whereas the United States was on the cutting edge of new developments and discoveries.

An America of Abundance

In the meantime, Americans were enjoying a spiritual spring after emerging from the harsh political winter of McCarthyism. Their newfound sense of freedom was being expressed most notably in a national love affair with the automobile, and President Dwight D. Eisenhower was establishing an interstate highway system on which Americans could drive them. The cars themselves reflected the nation's presumed advantage in the space race with the Soviets. Space rockets, once the stuff of science fiction, became the primary theme of automobile advertising. The Oldsmobile 88 car model, for example, was billed as the Rocket 88, and was pictured in front of a missile zooming skyward. In one advertisement for the Olds 88, a cartoon couple was pictured straddling a rocket. Decorative fins appeared on the rear of cars, calling to mind twin-tailed fighter jets, and the front grilles of cars were styled to resemble jet-engine intake ducts. Designers even installed protruding taillights on the fins, resembling flames from a jet afterburner.

In other areas as well, signs of abundance and confidence were plentiful and reflected the country's excitement about the space race they were sure they would win. The growing suburbs were furnished with ultramodern molded plastic chairs and eye-pleasing curved tables that drew part of their popularity from "space-age design." The nation's favorite color appeared to be pink, and almost any consumer good—typewriters, kitchen appliances, clothing, and even automobiles—could be found in pink. Meantime, Americans gobbled up heat-and-serve dishes and molded Jell-O salads. Television, which had helped expose McCarthy's shortcomings, was coming into its own as an entertainment medium. All in all, the period was one of optimism and plenty.

However, an unexpected development suddenly captured the nation's attention.

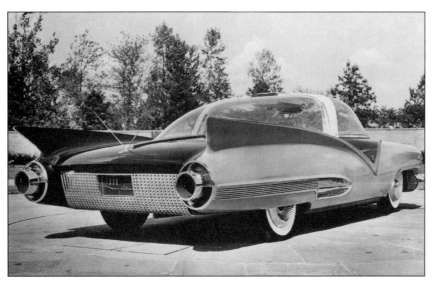

It became popular to design cars with characteristics similar to space rockets.

The Associated Press news service delivered the story to Americans in a dispatch which read, "LONDON, OCT. 4 (AP)—MOSCOW RADIO SAID TONIGHT THAT THE SOVIET UNION HAS LAUNCHED AN EARTH SATELLITE."[79] The Russians had beaten the United States into space. President Eisenhower tried to downplay the news, and that evening White House spokesman James Hagerty told reporters that, although "the Soviet satellite . . . is of great scientific interest," the development "did not come as any surprise; we have never thought of our program as in a race with the Soviets."[80]

A Mixed Reaction

Reaction to the Soviet achievement was generally mixed among Americans who that evening would be treated to the premier of the long running television series *Leave It to Beaver.* At a party at the Soviet embassy in Washington to which a number of American scientists involved in the International Geophysical Year project had been invited, the news was greeted with enthusiasm. American scientists congratulated their Soviet colleagues on the accomplishment, which was called *Sputnik,* Russian for "traveling companion of the Earth," or "fellow traveler." John Townsend Jr., an American scientist at the party, recalled, "My reaction was 'Damn!'"[81] In contrast, Senate Majority Leader Lyndon B. Johnson viewed the *Sputnik* launch with alarm. Johnson heard about *Sputnik* while hosting a barbeque at his Texas ranch. He walked the ranch and eyed the sky. "As we stood on the lonely country road that runs between our house and the Pedernales River, I felt uneasy and apprehensive. In the open West, you learn to live with the sky. It is a part of your life. But now, somehow, in some new way, the sky seemed almost alien,"[82] Johnson said. He added, "I also remember the profound shock of realizing that it might be possible for another nation to achieve technological superiority over this great country of ours."[83] For its part, *The New York Times* trumpeted the news with a rare three-line headline that ran across the entire top of the front page. It read:

SOVIET FIRES EARTH SATELLITE INTO SPACE; IT IS CIRCLING THE GLOBE AT 18,000 MPH; SPHERE TRACKED IN 4 CROSSINGS OVER U.S.[84]

Historian Doris Kearns Goodwin was in high school when she first heard of *Sputnik*. She and her boyfriend took a blanket to a nearby park to see whether they could spot the satellite. "And it was a very romantic setting, and we started to look for Sputnik. And then my boyfriend reached over and kissed me. . . . I didn't give Sputnik another thought,"[85] she recalled. Others were fascinated by the satellite. Saunders Kramer, a cofounder of the American Astronautical Society who was then working for the Lockheed Missiles and Space Company in California, got up early one morning to see if he could catch a glimpse of *Sputnik*. He later recalled that he questioned his sanity at the time, wondering, "What am I doing here, the only person crazy enough to be out here this early on a Saturday morning."[86] But within a few minutes, he realized he was not alone, as he could

Sputnik was the first satellite to be launched into space.

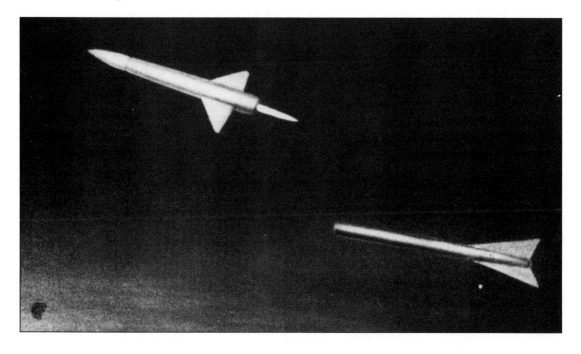

overhear neighbors asking, "Do you see it? Do you see it?"[87]

The nation's mixed reaction to *Sputnik* was in stark contrast to a steady drumbeat in the press about the potentially negative aspects of the Russian feat. *Newsweek* magazine, for example, in its October 14, 1957, issue warned,

> This achievement has been reached, in a torn world, by the controlled scientists of a despotic state—a state which had already given the word 'satellite' the implications of ruthless servitude. Could the crushers of Hungary be trusted with this new kind of satellite, whose implications no man could measure?[88]

For some Americans, the Soviet achievement was an eye-opener, revealing that the Soviet Union was not as technologically backward as many had believed. As one U.S. space scientist put it at the time, "The realization that the Russians weren't just a bunch of Tartars riding around on horseback out on the Siberian Steppes was brought home very vividly."[89] All the same, many Americans were unmoved by the development. *Newsweek*'s Boston correspondent reported "massive indifference,"[90] while one of the magazine's writers in Denver said in a memorandum that people there had "a vague feeling that we have stepped into a new era, but people aren't discussing it the way they are football and the Asiatic flu."[91] Some newspapers buried

the *Sputnik* launch on page three, as did the *Milwaukee Sentinel.* On page one, the paper read, "Today We Make History,"[92] a headline inspired by the fact that the city was for the first time hosting the World Series.

"We Will Bury You"

Americans, however, slowly came to understand *Sputnik*'s military implications. Although President Eisenhower, in an attempt to calm a slowly growing sense of public unease, said *Sputnik*'s success "does not raise my apprehensions, not one iota,"[93] many Americans were becoming deeply concerned. The *Sputnik* launch stirred fears of nuclear warheads being launched by the Soviets at the United States, or being rained on the United States from satellites in outer space. Soviet Premier Nikita Khrushchev had warned a year earlier that "History is on our side. We will bury you."[94] With those words fresh in many memories, Americans shuddered when Khrushchev, commenting on the success of *Sputnik*, declared that his country would be "turning out long-range missiles like sausages."[95]

Many critics began looking for a scapegoat for the nation's failure to beat the Soviets into space, and many concluded it was consumerism. Senator Styles Bridges took sharp aim at American society, declaring, "The time has come to be less concerned with the depth of pile on the new broadloom rug or the height of the tailfin on the new car and to be more prepared to shed blood, sweat and tears."[96] Although some Americans remained confident that the United States would soon launch its own satellite, and that it would be better than *Sputnik*, Senator Lyndon B. Johnson was cynical of such optimism. Of the possible improvements Americans might bring to satellite technology, Johnson quipped, "Perhaps it will even have chrome trim and automatic windshield wipers,"[97] a thinly veiled reference to what he perceived as Americans' attention to irrelevant detail. However, even before the United States attempted to get its first satellite aloft, the Soviets launched a second *Sputnik*, and this one carried a dog. Although technical problems ended up making a martyr of the dog, Laika, the second *Sputnik* sent a clear message. Weighing more than one thousand pounds—more than six times the first *Sputnik*—and carrying a living thing, observers could not help but conclude that the Soviets intended to put humans in space, and to do it quickly. The United States unquestionably was well behind the Soviet Union in space.

Johnson believed the stakes in this new game with the Soviets transcended the political and propaganda points the Soviets were winning around the world. He said,

Control of space means control of the world. From space the masters of infinity would have the power to control the earth's weather, to cause drought and flood, to change the tides and raise the levels of the sea, to divert the Gulf Stream and change temperate climates to frigid. That is the ultimate position: the position of total control over earth that lies somewhere in outer space.[98]

Vanguard Explodes

Finally, two months and two days after the Soviets launched the first *Sputnik*, the U.S. response, the *Vanguard*, was ready for launch. On December 6, 1957, all systems were ready. Then came disaster. A newspaper reporter assigned to cover the launch reported that *Vanguard* "rose less than five feet, toppled over, and exploded."[99] As recalled by Kurt Stehling, a German engineer who worked on the project:

It seemed as if the gates of hell had opened up. Brilliant stiletto flames shot out from the side of the rocket near the engine. The vehicle agonizingly hesitated for a moment, quivered again, and in front of our unbelieving, shocked eyes, began to topple. It sank like a great flaming sword into scabbard down into the blast tube. It toppled slowly, breaking apart, hitting part of the test guard and ground with a tremendous roar that could be felt and heard even behind the two-foot concrete wall of the blockhouse and the six-inch bulletproof glass. For a moment or two there was complete disbelief. I could

As an answer to Sputnik, *the United States attempted to launch the* Vanguard, *which exploded upon take-off.*

see it in the faces. I could feel it myself. This just couldn't be. . . . The fire died down and we saw America's supposed response to the 200-pound Soviet satellite—our four-pound grapefruit [a nickname given the satellite because of its small size]—lying amid the scattered glowing debris, still beeping away, unharmed.[100]

The *Vanguard* failure would be bitter for Americans, and newspapers around the world heralded the disaster. The *Louisville Courier-Journal* wryly noted, "A shot may be heard around the world, but there are times when a dud is even louder,"[101] while the *New York Herald Tribune* complained, "The people in Washington should damn well keep quiet until they have a grapefruit or at least something orbiting around up there."[102] But the biggest blow to American prestige came from Soviet gloating. At the United Nations, Soviet representatives offered to provide the United States with foreign aid under a Soviet program of technical assistance to underdeveloped nations, a dig at American smugness about its alleged technological superiority.

A new round of national soul-searching followed, and many concluded that America's educational system was to blame for the poor U.S. showing. In *Inside Russia Today*, John Gunther concluded that the Soviet Union had placed a higher priority on things that were important. He wrote:

The main emphasis is on science and technology, for both boys and girls.

In addition to ten solid years of arithmetic and mathematics, every child is obliged to take four years of chemistry, five of physics, and six of biology. Comparison to the United States is highly pertinent. Many American high schools have no physics or chemistry courses at all. An American authority told me that the Soviet child graduating from the tenth grade (our twelfth), aged about seventeen, has a better scientific education than most American *college* graduates. The average Russian boy or girl, taking the normal course, gets more than *five times* the amount of science and mathematics that is stipulated for entrance into Massachusetts Institute of Technology.[103]

A television documentary drove the point home by comparing the Soviet educational system, with its emphasis on the sciences, with a suburban high school in the United States. In the latter, the program showed American students taking such elective courses as coeducational cooking. Many Americans began to conclude that the United States would never catch up with the Soviets in space exploration unless the nation's educational system was improved.

The United States Enters the Race

Although it seemed like an agonizingly long time to many Americans, the United States eventually got into the race. Roughly two months after the *Vanguard*

SCORE One for Eisenhower

Although the United States had finally been able to successfully launch satellites into space, the first satellites were relatively light, especially when compared to the weight of Soviet satellites. As recalled in T.A. Heppenheimer's *Countdown: A History of Space Flight*, Soviet leader Nikita Khrushchev derisively said the United States would have to launch "very many satellites the size of oranges in order to catch up with the Soviet Union." Many in the United States agreed.

The United States slowly developed the ability to lift heavier satellites into space. In December 1958 an *Atlas* rocket was launched with two hundred pounds of radio communications equipment capable of retransmitting messages beamed from Earth or storing messages for later playback. The launch, called SCORE, contained a unique surprise for the world. From space orbit came the voice of President Dwight D. Eisenhower, who had recorded a message that was retransmitted back to Earth and could be heard on radios around the world. As Heppenheimer related in *Countdown*, Eisenhower's message was,

> This is the President of the United States speaking. Through the marvels of scientific advance my voice is coming to you from a satellite circling in outer space. My message is a simple one. Through this unique means I convey to you and to all mankind America's wish for peace on earth and good will toward men everywhere.

SCORE was a pioneering spacecraft that ushered in an age of satellite communications, which has since become a multibillion-dollar industry.

debacle, on January 31, 1958, an army *Jupiter* rocket launched the first U.S. satellite into orbit. While the successful launch

Van Allen Belts

Although it would take the United States until January 31, 1958, to get a satellite into space, the effort would be worth the wait—at least to scientists. As the *Explorer* satellite flew to a height in excess of one thousand five hundred miles above Earth, physicist James Van Allen monitored Geiger counters aboard the satellite that detected the number of electrically charged particles the craft came across in space.

Van Allen found an unexpectedly high number of charged particles trapped in the earth's magnetic field. The concentration of particles had actually been detected by equipment aboard the second *Sputnik*, but Soviet scientists did not immediately recognize the phenomenon. Van Allen, however, determined that the charged particles were concentrated in two belts surrounding Earth. Scientists later recognized that the charged particles could disrupt radio communications and therefore had to be taken into account in charting courses for satellites and in sending or receiving communications from satellites. The belts were named after Van Allen, and their discovery provided the United States with a needed ego boost after the nation's early difficulty in launching an Earth satellite.

bolstered the nation's faltering esteem, President Eisenhower wanted to soft-pedal the achievement because the U.S. program was still well behind the Soviets. When told the satellite, which was called *Explorer*, had gone into orbit, Eisenhower said simply: "That's wonderful. I sure feel a lot better now. Let's not make too big a hullabaloo over this."[104]

The troubled navy *Vanguard* would eventually get into orbit, and unlike the

Explorer or *Sputnik*, remains there today. Successfully launched on March 17, 1958, the Vanguard brought a number of innovations to rocketry. Among other things, it was the first ever to make use of solar energy, and it was the first to use solid-state devices and put into practice miniaturization, allowing the sleek satellite to cram a large amount of instruments into a small space. Among *Vanguard*'s contributions to science was the data it sent back proving a long-held theory that the Earth is slightly pear-shaped, and that a satellite's orbit is affected by a variety of factors ranging from solar wind to the Earth's magnetic field. Originally believed to have a two-hundred-year lifespan, *Vanguard* is now expected to stay aloft anywhere between one thousand and two thousand more years. It is the oldest man-made object in space.

The *Explorer* and *Vanguard* launches reinvigorated the nation's sense of confidence, but Eisenhower knew that in order for the nation to move ahead in the realm of space exploration, the United States would need to sharpen its focus. During a joint session of Congress on April 2, 1958, the president urged creation of a civilian National Aeronautics and Space Administration, or NASA. Congress responded quickly, and NASA was up and running by October 1. Just one week later, NASA administrator T. Keith Glennan approved a plan to work on manned space exploration under a program called Project Mercury. By 1960

NASA had developed a ten-year plan that called for the launch of a variety of satellites, moon probes, and manned flights in Earth orbit and around the moon.

"What Can We Do?"

The space race was rapidly picking up in pace, but the United States seemed to be chronically behind. On November 21,

---

On April 12, 1961, Yuri Gagarin became the first man to travel into space.

1960, a test of a rocket that scientists hoped would launch Americans into space was unable to lift itself off the launch pad. Then on April 12, 1961, Soviet Yuri Gagarin took an eighty-nine-minute flight in the earth's orbit, becoming the first person in history to travel into space. Once again the national mood soured. Whereas Americans had a proud history of aeronautical firsts, ranging from the Wright Brothers' success in building the first workable airplane and Charles A. Lindbergh's historic transatlantic flight in the *Spirit of Saint Louis*, the Soviets always seemed to be the first in space.

Shortly into his presidency, John F. Kennedy brainstormed possible ways to finally get the United States into the space race lead. Meeting with advisers on the day of Gagarin's space first, Kennedy was dismayed at the state of the nation's space program. "We may never catch up,"[105] he fretted. Looking for any area in which the United States might excel, Kennedy asked, "Is there any place where we can catch them? What can we do? Can we go around the moon before them? Can we put a man on the moon before them?"[106] After being told that a crash program might allow the United States to be the first to orbit the moon or achieve a moon landing, at a cost of $40 billion, Kennedy initially balked, saying he needed more

Kennedy Pushes for a Lead in the Space Race

While President John F. Kennedy fretted about the Soviet Union's lead in the space race, he turned to his vice president, Lyndon B. Johnson, in a search for ways the United States could catch up and surpass the Soviets. Johnson, who as a member of the Senate had taken an active interest in the space program, was chairman of the president's space council.

As reprinted in *Footprints on the Moon*, by the writers and editors of The Associated Press, Kennedy drafted a memorandum to Johnson on April 20, 1961, that read:

MEMORANDUM FOR THE VICE PRESIDENT

In accordance with our conversation I would like for you as Chairman of the Space Council to be in charge of making an over-all survey of where we stand in space.

1. Do we have a chance of beating the Soviets by putting a laboratory in space, or by a trip around the moon, or by a rocket to land on the moon, or by a rocket to go to the moon and back with a man? Is there any other space program which promises dramatic results in which we could win?

2. How much additional will it cost?

3. Are we working 24 hours a day on existing programs? If not, why not? If not, will you make recommendations to me as to how work can be speeded up.

4. In building large boosters, should we put our emphasis on nuclear, chemical or liquid fuel, or a combination of the three?

5. Are we making maximum effort? Are we achieving necessary results? I have asked . . . responsible officials to cooperate with you fully. I would appreciate a report on this at the earliest possible moment.

JOHN F. KENNEDY

Johnson provided a preliminary report to Kennedy on April 28 and a final report May 8. With the Johnson response as a guide, Kennedy on May 25 committed the United States to landing men on the moon and returning them to Earth.

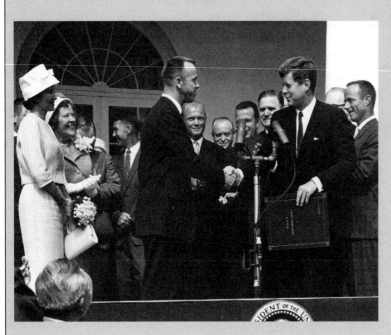

President Kennedy shakes the hand of the first American to fly into space, Alan B. Shepard Jr.

information before he could decide whether the cost would be worth the return. As discussion continued, however, Kennedy indicated that the United States sorely needed to surpass the Soviets in space, regardless of cost. "If somebody can tell me just how to catch up. Let's find somebody—anybody. I don't care if it's the janitor over there, if he knows how," Kennedy said, adding, "There's nothing more important."[107]

As the Kennedy administration mulled its options, astronaut Alan Shepard took a fifteen-minute suborbital ride on May 5, 1961, the first U.S. manned foray into space. Although it could scarcely compare with Gagarin's earlier achievement, the flight put the United States back into the race. Kennedy, bolstered by the success of Shepard's flight, on May 25 outlined an ambitious agenda for the nation's space program.

Kennedy Commits United States to Moon Landing

Speaking before a joint session of Congress, Kennedy made a broad-ranging speech that covered a waterfront of issues confronting the nation from disarmament to civil rights. Tucked within was a bold challenge. Kennedy said:

> Now is the time to take longer strides—time for a great new American enterprise—time for this nation to take a clearly leading role in space achievement, which in many ways may hold the key to our future on earth. . . .

> I believe this nation should commit itself to achieving the goal, before the decade is out, of landing a man on the moon and returning him safely to earth. No single space project in this period will be more impressive to mankind, or more important for the long-range exploration of space; and none will be so difficult or expensive to accomplish.[108]

Invigorated with a new sense of purpose, NASA methodically worked to meet Kennedy's goal. In Project Mercury, NASA launched a series of manned flights that were designed to test the effects of both suborbital and orbital flights on men and rockets. Under the Mercury program, astronaut John Glenn became the first American to orbit the earth, doing so three times in a capsule called *Friendship 7*, traveling eighty-one thousand miles in a flight that lasted four hours, fifty-five minutes, and twenty-three seconds. The second stage of the moon effort was called Project Gemini, in which two-man teams maneuvered spacecraft to rendezvous and link up with other spacecraft. A highlight of the Gemini program was *Gemini 4*, in which astronaut Ed White made a twenty-minute space walk, the first by an American, on June 3, 1965. The final stage of the NASA effort was Project Apollo, which eventually culminated in the realization of Kennedy's challenge.

Apollo, however, would begin much as the American space program itself—in

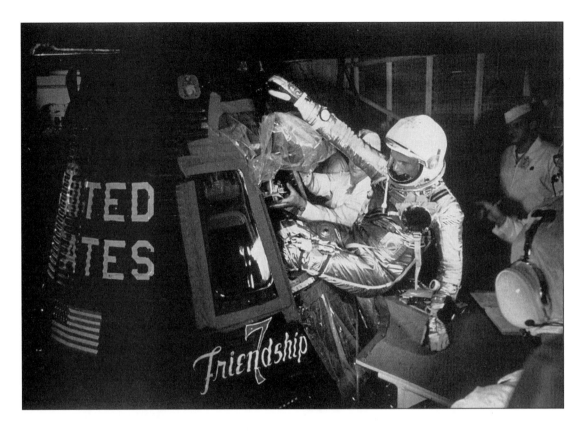

Climbing into the Friendship 7, John Glenn was about to become the first U.S. man to orbit Earth.

fiery disaster. On January 27, 1967, astronauts Virgil I. Grissom, Edward H. White, and Roger B. Chaffee were conducting a practice countdown three weeks prior to their scheduled takeoff. A fire, believed to have been caused by faulty wiring that set off a spark in the oxygen-rich environment of the capsule, exploded in the cabin. The three astronauts died, and the Apollo program was delayed for twenty-one months as engineers labored to make safety improvements. By December 21, 1968, however, NASA was nearing the finish line. On that day *Apollo 8* lifted off on an historic mission that NASA rocket ex-

pert Wernher von Braun labeled "man's first step away from this abode to another heavenly body."[109] Propelled by a powerful *Saturn 5* rocket that drank fifteen tons of fuel a second, *Apollo 8* orbited the earth 118 miles skyward in less than twelve minutes from launch. Traveling at 17,400 miles per hour, *Apollo 8*'s astronauts fired another set of engines that took the craft into orbit around the moon. Then on May 18, 1969, the *Apollo*

10 mission featured the final rehearsal for a moon landing, when a lunar module nicknamed Snoopy came within nine miles of touching down on the moon.

"The Eagle Has Landed"

The world stood transfixed by the *Apollo 11* mission. It lifted off at 9:32 A.M. on July 16, 1969. One hundred two hours and forty-six minutes later, the world learned that the lunar module nicknamed the *Eagle* had reached its destination when astronaut Neil Armstrong radioed the message: "The Eagle has landed."[110] Just eight years after President Kennedy had challenged the nation to land a man on the moon, Americans were now there. At Mission Control in Houston, the news was greeted with undisguised relief. "We copy you on the ground. You've got a bunch of guys about to turn blue. We're breathing again. Thanks a lot."[111] But as astonishing as the thought of actually landing on the moon, more drama was yet to come. As Mike Collins orbited the moon in the space capsule Columbia, astronauts Neil Armstrong and Edwin

(Buzz) Aldrin readied themselves for their historic mission. People around the world hovered around television screens when six and a half hours after landing on the moon, Armstrong opened the hatch and descended a ladder. The world-wide audience listened in as Armstrong chatted with Mission Control:

In July 1969, Astronaut Neil Armstrong (below) became the first man to walk on the moon.

Houston: Okay, Neill, we can see you coming down the ladder.

Armstrong: I'm at the foot of the ladder. I'm going to step off the [lunar module] now. That's one small step for a man, one giant leap for mankind.[112]

Aldrin later joined Armstrong on the moon, and the two undertook a variety of experiments and collected lunar samples. Then at close to midnight, the astronauts were interrupted by Mission Control with a phone call patched through from Washington. President Richard M. Nixon called the astronauts from the Oval Office, saying, "I just can't tell you how proud we all are. For every American, this has to be the proudest day of our lives. And for people all over the world, I am sure they, too, join with Americans, in recognizing what a feat this is. Because of what you have done, the heavens have become a part of man's world."[113]

When the astronauts returned to Earth on July 24, Nixon was there to greet them. "This is the greatest week in the history of the world since the Creation," he said. "As a result of what you have done, the world has never been closer together."[114]

Impact of the Space Program

Like Nixon, Americans gloried in the nation's space triumph. Astronauts became heroes, schoolchildren aspired to be astronauts, and the number of Americans studying engineering, science, and mathematics at the nation's colleges skyrocketed. Americans also enjoyed a number of consumer spin-offs from the space program. Critics sometimes allege that for its billions of dollars of investment in space, the United States got only "Teflon, Tang and Velcro"[115] in return. The critics are actually in error, because those three products, though utilized by the space program, were actually developed for other uses. Teflon was developed by the DuPont chemical company in 1938 and was used by NASA in space suits and nose cones. Tang was developed by General Foods for army field rations and became a consumer product that NASA later used for Apollo Program astronauts. Finally, Velcro was invented in 1948 by a Swiss engineer, and NASA used the product to hold items in place in the zero gravity of space. However, the space program did develop a host of products and technology that have had an enormous effect on daily life. As just one example, communications satellites were born of a 1961 NASA program. By 1965 the communications satellite industry became commercial and is now a multibillion-dollar industry that has helped to make possible the widespread use of wireless phones.

Likewise, the Internet can trace its birth to the space program. Scientists and researchers around the nation needed a network that would allow them to share mainframe computers for their work on the space program. The forerunner of today's global Internet was called ARPANET, which at its inception in 1969 linked the University of California at Los Angeles, Stanford Research Instititute, the University of California at Santa Barbara, and the University of Utah.

A host of other less spectacular, but important, products now in daily use were initially developed for the space program. For example, Kevlar, a tough, fireproof fabric, was developed for use in space suits and today is used to make bulletproof vests. Guidance systems developed for use in space are now in commercial jets and are one tool used by meteorologists to track hurricanes.

Freeze-dried food, solar panels, and composite graphite (developed for space use and now used for sporting equipment ranging from tennis rackets to golf clubs) are other examples of products that resulted from the space program.

The tense competition with the Soviet Union in space exploration was in many respects a proxy for war, and in the end, the United States was victorious. However, the Cold War backdrop against which the space race took place always contained an edginess about it, because the threat of a hot war never seemed far from the surface. That threat led to the growth of ever-expanding military expenditures that ultimately would dwarf the cost of the moon program.

Chapter 5

The Military-Industrial Complex

Even as the United States was engaged in its high-profile space race with the Soviet Union, a profound change was occurring in the way national leaders viewed the nation's defense. Spurred by distress about what appeared to be the increasing likelihood of nuclear war, and the Soviet Union's stated goal of achieving world domination, the U.S. government began to encourage the growth of a permanent defense industry. Once rooted, the defense industry grew exponentially, bringing the nation enormous economic benefits even as it so skewed the nation's economy that money was not available for worthwhile nondefense projects.

A Positive Economic Stimulus

Almost instantly, the nation's economy—and American workers—benefited from defense spending. From 1947 to 1992 the United States spent more than $10 trillion on defense, which through the years provided millions of Americans with well-paying jobs. Although many defense industry employees had misgivings about their work, knowing that if the weapons they made were ever used millions of people could perish, they also enjoyed the income and job security the industry provided. Millions of other American workers benefited from defense spending indirectly as those employed in the defense industry spent their paychecks, stimulating job growth in other sectors of the economy.

The ever-escalating defense budget provided an enormous stimulus to the economy, and the U.S. Congress found it difficult to rein in spending. The United States spent close to $82 billion on defense in 1970, a figure that would climb to $300 billion in 1990. In 1987 the United States spent $8.7 billion on the nation's nuclear weapons program—which was made up of three government-owned weapons laboratories, nine factories, and seven assembly facilities, which employed more than one hundred thousand people. Private-sector firms received an even greater share of defense dollars. In 1990 alone, these companies won government contracts worth in excess of $121 billion. Both the military and companies within the defense industry honeycombed the nation with bases, factories, and research facilities. Those institutions, in turn, provided jobs for large numbers of Americans.

The union between the military and its defense contractors became known as the military-industrial complex, its power evidenced by the reluctance of Congress to limit defense spending. Not wishing to put large numbers of their constituents out of work, members of Congress routinely funded programs and weapons systems that in many cases were of questionable value. As noted by journalist William Greider, "If a new bomber of dubious purpose were being rolled out for production, it helped that hundreds of congressional districts were building pieces of it."[116]

World War III Feared

The increased defense spending was born of very real consternation following World War II that the Soviet Union was intent upon launching war against the United States. General Lucius Clay, the U.S. military governor in Germany, told President Truman in 1948 that he believed the Soviet Union was preparing for war, and he warned that World War III "may come

with dramatic suddenness."[117] Clay's message sent a chill throughout Washington, and by year's end President Truman's National Security Council had adopted its first classified order regarding the use of atomic weapons. In the order, NSC-30, the military was told it "must be ready to utilize promptly and effectively all appropriate means available, including atomic weapons, in the interest of national security and must plan accordingly."[118]

To implement NSC-30, the Strategic Air Command, an air force unit, was established to be constantly ready for war anywhere in the world. Lieutenant General Curtis E. LeMay assumed command of the operation in October 1948 and began a practice that became common during the Cold War. He amassed a large stockpile of nuclear weapons—smaller, lighter, and more powerful than those first used against Japan. No matter how many weapons of mass destruction he had, LeMay wanted more. By the end of 1949 LeMay envisioned a blistering U.S. nuclear onslaught against any Communist aggression—an onslaught so widespread it would destroy not only military targets, but entire Communist countries.

LeMay's battle plan was greeted with alarm by some military officials. Navy admiral Daniel Gallery, for example, noted that "Leveling large cities has a tendency to alienate the affections of the inhabitants and does not create an atmosphere of international good will after the war," adding that LeMay's plan was "an unworthy

Chief of Staff of the United States, General Marshall (above) sits at his desk in the War Department.

one for a country of our strength."[119] Navy rear admiral Ralph A. Ofstie said the plan amounted to nothing more than "the wholesale extermination of civilians" and was therefore "ruthless and barbaric."[120]

Nevertheless, U.S. scientists were at the same time laboring to create ever more destructive weapons, including the hydrogen, or Super, bomb. Thousands of other Americans found jobs in the economy's ever-expanding defense sector, whose growth was spurred by increasingly bleak assessments of Soviet intentions. "We must realize that we are now in a

mortal conflict. It is not a cold war; it is a hot war,"[121] warned Deputy Defense Secretary Robert Levitt in a thinly veiled appeal for a larger defense budget.

An Escalating Threat

Even though ever-increasing amounts of money were being poured into the military, top government officials continued to worry about what the United States regarded as an escalating Soviet threat. At the end of January 1950, Truman asked the National Security Council to appraise the nation's international affairs program. The top-secret document, known as NSC-68, was delivered to Truman on April 7, 1950. It warned that "the Soviet Union, unlike previous aspirants to hegemony, is animated by a new fanatic faith, antithetical to our own, and seeks to impose its absolute authority over the rest of the world."[122] The document went on to state that at stake in the battle between the United States and USSR was nothing less than "the fulfillment or destruction not only of this Republic but of civilization itself."[123] According to the security council document:

The Kremlin regards the United States as the only major threat to the achievement of its fundamental design. There is a basic conflict between the idea of freedom under a government of laws, and the idea of slavery under the grim oligarchy of the Kremlin, which has come to a crisis with the polarization of power . . . and the exclusive possession of atomic weapons by the two protagonists. . . .

A Death Star Named MILSTAR

During the height of Cold War tensions, the U.S. military searched for improved ways of ensuring the United States could wage and win a nuclear war. One idea, which never came to fruition, was the Military Strategic, Tactical, and Relay system, or MILSTAR, which would have been made up of a series of linked satellites. Its sole function would have been to serve as a computerized system to fight and win a nuclear war, and to do so even if the U.S. chain of command had been destroyed by a Soviet nuclear attack.

According to Tim Weiner in *Blank Check: The Pentagon's Black Budget*, MILSTAR's job would have been to win a nuclear war, and perhaps even two, even if there were no survivors in the United States. He wrote that MILSTAR was envisioned as a way to keep on firing nuclear weapons "without a human mind to direct it, for months on end, until the final missile screams across the sky." Weiner added, however, that though millions of dollars had been spent in preliminary work on the program, it was never implemented. He wrote, "The system has not been built because no one has the slightest notion of how to do it. The challenge has confounded the leading military minds of two generations."

Thus unwillingly our free society finds itself mortally challenged by the Soviet system. No other value system is so wholly irreconcilable with ours, so implacable in its purpose to destroy ours, so capable of turning to its own uses the most dangerous and divisive trends in our own society, no other so skillfully and powerfully evokes the elements of irrationality in human nature everywhere, and no other has the support of a great and growing center of military power.[124]

The analysis concluded that the United States had no choice but to undertake a rapid mobilization of the political, economic, and military strength of Western non-Communist nations in an effort to either forestall war or to be prepared for a conflict launched by the Soviets. The NSC report said the United States and its allies had to be strong militarily in order

to wrest the initiative from the Soviet Union, confront it with convincing evidence of the determination and ability of the free world to frustrate the Kremlin design of a world dominated by its will. Such evidence is the only means short of war which eventually may force the Kremlin to abandon its present course of action.[125]

According to the report, the nation's military strength was inadequate in the face of a growing Soviet threat, and nothing short of a crash course would be necessary. "Budgetary considerations will need to be subordinated to the stark fact that our very independence as a nation may be at stake,"[126] the report said.

Defense Spending Skyrockets

The government heeded the security council's call, and military spending shot up from $13.7 billion in 1950 to $52.8 billion in 1953. Although the United States had entered the Korean War in 1950, less than 10 percent of the increased defense spending went to that conflict. The rest was put into strategic armaments. When LeMay first assumed control of the Strategic Air Command, he had roughly thirty bombers equipped with nuclear weapons. By 1953 he had more than one thousand at his disposal. LeMay was not the only one who benefited from the increased spending, however, as many other Americans also enjoyed high-paying jobs making parts for and assembling the nation's war machines.

Although President Eisenhower continued Truman's policy of escalating defense expenditures, he expressed grave misgivings about the practice because of hidden costs to society. As he said in one speech, "The worst to be feared and the best to be expected can be simply stated. The worst is atomic war. The best would be this: a life of perpetual fear and tension; a burden of arms draining the wealth and labor of all peoples."[127] He added:

Every warship launched, every rocket fired signifies, in the final sense, a theft from those who hunger and are not fed, those who are cold and are not clothed. The cost of one modern heavy bomber is this: a modern brick school in more than thirty cities. It is two electric power plants, each serving a city of sixty thousand population. It is two fine, fully equipped hospitals. . . . This is not a way of life at all, in any true sense. Under the cloud of threatening war, it is humanity hanging from a cross of iron.[128]

Eisenhower ultimately became so concerned about the costs of defending the nation—both in terms of money spent and in opportunities lost to enrich the nation's way of life—he seriously considered the possibility of attacking the Soviet Union as a way to put an end to the escalating arms race. When the Soviet Union exploded its first hydrogen bomb in August 1953, Secretary of State John Foster Dulles suggested the time to attack may have arrived. "Sooner or later we must manage to remove the taboo from the use of these weapons,"[129] he said. By September, Eisenhower was thinking along the same lines. He wrote Dulles that continued weapons spending threatened to bankrupt the nation. "The cost would either drive us to war—or into some form of dictatorial government. In such circumstances, we would be forced to consider whether or not our duty to future genera-

President Eisenhower increased spending on the manufacturing of weapons, and factories like the one seen above began mass-producing missiles.

tions did not require us to *initiate* war at the most propitious moment."[130]

Eisenhower Warns of the Military-Industrial Complex

Eisenhower ultimately rejected the idea, realizing that bombing the Soviets with nuclear weapons as a solution to the arms race had monumental humanitarian and practical drawbacks. Speaking to the Joint Chiefs of Staff in 1954, he noted that a nuclear strike by the United States would level the Soviet Union and Eastern Europe. "I ask you what would the civilized world do about it? I repeat there is no victory except through our imaginations."[131] Eisenhower also realized any nuclear attack by the United States would produce such massive radioactive fallout that the United States would be jeopardized, even forgetting the real likelihood of a massive Soviet nuclear response. "There just might be nothing left of the Northern Hemisphere,"[132] he mused to a national security assistant in 1959.

A year later, as he prepared to leave office, Eisenhower remained troubled about the escalating arms race, especially after he reviewed the Strategic Air Command's nuclear war battle plan. Called the Single Integrated Operational Plan, or SIOP, the plan called for the United States to launch 3,267 nuclear warheads against the Soviet Union, China, and Eastern Europe in the event of hostilities with the Soviet Union. Thousands more nuclear bombs would be launched against those nations in subsequent strikes, until the U.S. arsenal was spent. The plan envisioned the complete annihilation of ten countries and the deaths of 500 million people. Despite being shaken by the nation's battle plan, Eisenhower nevertheless believed the nation had to be prepared for such a war. In his farewell speech to the nation, Eisenhower said the nation's military had to "be mighty, ready for instant action, so that no potential aggressor may be tempted to risk his own destruction."[133] Eisenhower also vented the frustrations the arms race had caused him. He said:

Until the latest of our world conflicts, the United States had no armaments industry. American makers of plowshares could, with time and as required, make swords as well. But now we can no longer risk emergency improvisation of national defense; we have been compelled to create a permanent armaments industry of vast proportions. Added to this, three and a half million men and women are directly engaged in the defense establishment. We annually spend on military security more than the net income of all United States corporations.[134]

According to Eisenhower, the influence of the arms race extended throughout all aspects of American life and posed the danger of placing too much power in the hands of those involved in the nation's defense. In a passage that would first give the name military-industrial complex to the close association between the military and its contractors, he warned, "In the councils of government, we must guard against the acquisition of unwarranted influence, whether sought or unsought, by the military-industrial complex. The potential for the disastrous rise of misplaced power exists and will persist."[135]

Likewise, Eisenhower saw danger in the fact that the nation's technological and scientific thinking had been harnessed almost completely by the military and defense industry. Eisenhower said that, in his view, too much of the nation's scientific research was being done solely on defense projects. He added:

Today, the solitary inventor, tinkering in his shop, has been overshadowed by task forces of scientists in laboratories and testing fields. In the same fashion, the free university, historically the fountainhead of free ideas

Eisenhower's New Look

When President Dwight D. Eisenhower came into office in 1953, he wanted to put a limit on defense expenditures. The World War II hero figured he could achieve savings by cutting back on conventional forces, and instead rely on nuclear weapons. To Eisenhower the choice was simple. A ton of TNT cost one thousand seven hundred dollars in 1953, while atomic weapons could create an explosion of similar size for twenty-three dollars.

By the fall of 1953 Eisenhower had approved a National Security Council directive that came to be known as the "New Look." As reproduced in Allan M. Winkler's *The Cold War: A History in Documents*, the directive asserted that:

> Within the free world, only the United States can provide and maintain, for a period of years to come, the atomic capability to counterbalance Soviet atomic power. Thus, sufficient atomic weapons and effective means of delivery are indispensable for U.S. security. Moreover, in the face of Soviet atomic power, defense of the continental United States becomes vital to effective se-

curity: to protect our striking force, our mobilization base, and our people. Such atomic capability is also a major contribution to the security of our allies, as well as of this country . . . . In the event of hostilities, the United States will consider nuclear weapons to be as available for use as other munitions.

Eisenhower's Secretary of State explained the policy of utilizing nuclear weapons as being based on the concept of deterrence. As Winkler recounts in *The Cold War*, Dulles said:

> We want, for ourselves and the other free nations, a maximum deterrent at a bearable cost. Local defense will always be important. But there is no local defense which alone will contain the mighty land power of the Communist world. Local defenses must be reinforced by the further deterrent of massive retaliatory power. . . . The way to deter aggression is for the free community to be willing and able to respond vigorously at places and with means of its own choosing.

and scientific discovery, has experienced a revolution in the conduct of research. Partly because of the huge costs involved, a government contract becomes virtually a substitute for intellectual curiosity. For every old blackboard there are now hundreds of new electric computers.[136]

A Perplexing Problem

Eisenhower's parting words were chilling. Not only did he leave the impression that

the public needed to keep a closer eye on the military, he said the nation's priorities had been perverted by the competition between the United States and USSR. Although his own policies had contributed to the growth of a permanent defense industry, Eisenhower was fearful of what such policies had wrought. It had, in effect, skewed the nation's priorities away from pure science to work on finding ever more efficient means of killing. The mounting defense expenditures were siphoning money and intellectual brainpower that otherwise might be devoted to finding cures for diseases, enhancing humankind's understanding of the world and universe, or improving life in myriad other ways.

The issue posed a vexing riddle, however. As Eisenhower pointed out, millions of workers were directly involved in defense industry work. Hundreds of thousands of other workers were indirectly involved, examining and developing technologies that could be brought to bear in the escalating arms race. Although their work could bring mass death of an unimaginable scale, the workers themselves were enjoying unprecedented wealth.

After the shortages and deprivations of the Great Depression and World War II, Americans were making up for lost time, and on a grand scale. A staple photograph of American news magazines was a picture showing an American family surrounded by all the groceries it would consume in a typical year. Abundance was not limited to food, however. Americans were purchasing all types of appliances, from refrigerators to washing machines, and increasingly these items were offered in an array of colors and styles. Even such items as women's nylons, which had been in short supply during World War II, had begun to be offered in a variety of colors. Government expenditures on weapons of mass destruction were helping to fuel an unprecedented economic boom.

In the 1950s Americans increased their spending, and began buying pricey items like refrigerators.

Lost Opportunities?

The nation's affluence had Cold War implications. Sociologist David Riesman, only partly in jest, had suggested that instead of a Cold War with the Soviet Union, the

"And We Call Ourselves the Human Race"

When President John F. Kennedy was first shown the nation's nuclear war plan—the Single Integrated Operational Plan, or SIOP—shortly after he took office, he was told the plan offered little flexibility. Moreover, scaling back the number of nuclear missiles launched would mean little in humanitarian terms because any nuclear assault on the Soviet Union would still kill millions of civilians. According to Tim Weiner in *Blank Check: The Pentagon's Black Budget*, Kennedy left the meeting disgusted and complained to Secretary of State Dean Rusk, "And we call ourselves the human race."

Kennedy then sought to rethink the nation's nuclear war policy. A more flexible approach than the first SIOP was developed, allowing limited use of nuclear weapons. A five-prong strategy was ultimately developed, a series of steadily escalating options leading to all-out nuclear war. However, when confronted with the Cuban missile crisis—when the Soviet Union in 1962 began to install nuclear weapons in Cuba, an uncomfortably short distance from the United States—Kennedy and his advisers came to see that even a limited nuclear confrontation carried with it costs too great to risk. From then on, people both inside and out of government began to question the rationale underlying America's defense posture. Built on the notion of attaining and maintaining superiority over the Soviet nuclear arsenal, the plan had serious flaws in the minds of many Americans. Weiner recounts that Kennedy himself asked during the height of the Cuban missile crisis, "What difference does it make? They've got enough to blow us up now anyway." Similar feelings would plague later presidential administrations. As Weiner relates in *Blank Check*, President Richard M. Nixon's secretary of state, Henry Kissinger, asked in 1974, "What in the name of God is strategic superiority? What is the significance of it politically, militarily, operationally at these levels of numbers? What do you do with it?"

United States should launch a "nylon war."[137] His reasoning was that, if the United States were to inundate the Soviet Union with women's hosiery, home permanent kits, lipstick, cooking ranges, and freezers, the Soviet Union would be forced to abandon the arms race and focus its efforts on "consumers' goods, or face mass discontent on an increasing scale."[138] Detractors, however, saw a shallowness and frivolity in what had come to be called the American Dream. Novelist and social critic John Steinbeck in 1959 wrote that he detected in mass consumerism the "creeping, all-pervading nerve gas of immorality," adding that, "If I wanted to destroy a nation, I would give it too [many material goods] and I would have it on its knees, miserable, greedy and sick."[139] Nevertheless, no one seriously argued for a Soviet-style system that produced clunky, unfashionable, and undependable consumer goods that the average consumer could not afford to purchase.

At the same time, no one likewise could say what truly important advances in science and technology were being passed over in an economy that focused on building ever more horrible weapons.

Even well after Eisenhower left office, some policy makers worried about the skewed priorities of the arms race. The National Science Board in 1992, for example, issued a report showing that between 1980 and 1989, the United States, Japan, and West Germany each spent about the same percentage of gross national product (GNP)—the total value of all goods and services produced in a nation during a year—on research and development. However, the United States during that time spent less on nondefense research and development compared to Japan and West Germany's expenditures on nondefense research. Analysts worried that, because the United States devoted less effort toward developing new technologies, products, and medicines than other countries, the nation and its economy could suffer as a result.

Eisenhower's conundrum about a military-industrial complex would remain just that, as successive presidents found it impossible to cut defense spending because of the supposedly continuing Soviet threat and because of the stimulating effect defense spending had on the U.S. economy. In 1980, for example, the Soviet Union spent an estimated $1,096 on defense for every man, woman, and child in that nation. The United States, by contrast, spent $931 per capita (person) on defense. Driven by the fear that the Soviets might gain a competitive military advantage, the United States by 1989 had increased its per capita expenditures to $1,222, eclipsing the $1,077 spent by the Soviet Union. Americans, meantime, continued to benefit from the expenditures through defense industry jobs.

The peacetime mobilization of the nation's manufacturing sector led to the growth of a permanent defense industry so entrenched that it would be difficult to dismantle. Although fueled in large measure by fears that the Soviet Union was gearing up to destroy the United States under a blizzard of nuclear warheads, the escalating arms race between the two nations was further complicated in the United States by the fact that so many Americans relied on defense spending for their way of life. At the same time, however, a substantial number of Americans had grown to view the nation's atomic arsenal not as a protector of freedom and source of jobs, but as a prison. Worries about a nuclear Armageddon planted the seeds for a broad-based antinuclear movement.

Chapter 6

"Mankind Is Doomed"

hroughout the length of the Cold War, a significant number of Americans raised their voices in protest against atomic and nuclear weapons. Even some scientists involved in their creation came to see the weapons as needlessly destructive and a threat to all life on earth. Many average citizens joined in protest, spawning a grassroots ban-the-bomb movement.

Atomic Scientists Work to Limit Atomic Weapons

Some atomic scientists were the first to raise alarms about the pure power of the atom bomb. When the United States first tested the atomic bomb in 1945, physicist J. Robert Oppenheimer, the leader of the Manhattan Project, was moved to quote a passage from Hindu scripture. Drawing from the *Bhagavad Gita*, Oppenheimer recited, "If the radiance of a thousand suns were to burst into the sky, that would be like the splendor of the Mighty One. . . . I

am become Death, destroyer of worlds."[140] Just months after the United States dropped atom bombs on Japan, a number of American physicists formed a group called the Federation of Atomic Scientists. Later renamed the Federation of American Scientists, the group launched a fruitless effort to place strict limits on the growth of atomic weapons.

Four years later, Oppenheimer was the chairman of an advisory group that urged President Truman not to pursue creation of an even more powerful hydrogen bomb. The committee said such weapons would be tools that would be good for only one thing—killing vast numbers of civilians. "The fact that no limits exist to the destructiveness of this weapon makes its very existence and the knowledge of its construction a danger to humanity as a whole. It is necessarily an evil thing considered in any light,"[141] the panel told Truman. Truman, however, dismissed Oppenheimer as "a crybaby"[142]

Albert Einstein and the Bomb

In 1939 Albert Einstein, the brilliant physicist, was concerned. As scientists in the United States conducted experiments to see whether it would be possible to split atoms and possibly create a bomb powerful enough to level entire cities, many in the scientific community were worried that Hitler's Germany was on the same track. Such a development, they feared, would allow Hitler to achieve his goal of global conquest. Einstein shared those fears, and agreed to write President Franklin Delano Roosevelt to urge him to launch a major project to harness atomic power for the use of the United States.

As reprinted in Allan M. Winkler's *The Cold War: A History in Documents,* Einstein in a letter dated August 2, 1939, wrote to Roosevelt:

Some recent work by E. Fermi and L. Szilard, which has been communicated to me in manuscript, leads me to expect that the element uranium may be turned into a new and important source of energy in the immediate future. Certain aspects of the situation which has arisen seem to call for watchfulness and, if necessary, quick action on the part of the Administration. I believe therefore that it is my duty to bring to your attention the following facts and recommendations:

In the course of the last four months it has been made probable—through the work of Joliot in France as well as Fermi and Szilard in America—that it may become possible to set up a nuclear chain reaction in a large mass of uranium, by which vast amounts of power and large quantities of new radium-like elements would be generated. Now it appears almost certain that this could be achieved in the immediate future.

This new phenomenon would also lead to the construction of bombs, and it is conceivable—though much less certain—that extremely powerful bombs of a new type may thus be constructed. A single bomb of this type, carried by boat and exploded in a port, might very well destroy the whole port together with some of the surrounding territory. However, such bombs might very well prove to be too heavy for transportation by air.

The United States has only very poor ores of uranium in moderate quantities. There is some good ore in Canada and the former Czechoslovakia, while the most important source of uranium is Belgian Congo.

In view of this situation you may think it desirable to have some permanent contact maintained between the Administration and the group of physicists working on chain reactions in America.

A receptive Roosevelt was so intrigued by Einstein's proposal he established the Manhattan Project. For his part, though, Einstein regretted the letter the rest of his life. Following the war Einstein worked to ban atomic and nuclear weapons. As recounted by Winkler, Einstein said, "I made one great mistake in my life, when I signed the letter to President Roosevelt recommending that atom bombs be made, but there was some justification—the danger that the Germans would make them."

and told aides he did not want to see Oppenheimer ever again.

Not to be deterred, the brilliant scientist Albert Einstein, whose seminal work had paved the way for development of atomic weapons, warned that the explosive power of such bombs was only part of their danger. On February 12, 1950, he warned that "Radioactive poisoning of the atmosphere and hence annihilation of any life on earth has been brought within the range of technical possibilities. . . . In the end, there beckons more and more clearly general annihilation."[143]

A Movement Is Born

Americans came to understand Einstein's warning after a mishap occurred during a 1954 U.S. test of the hydrogen bomb in the Pacific Ocean. Radioactive plumes from the blast spread more widely than expected. When they settled on the crew of the *Lucky Dragon*, a Japanese fishing boat, crew members quickly became ill, and one died within six months. Atomic Energy Commission Chairman Lewis Strauss at first claimed the Japanese boat was actually a "Red spy outfit. If I were the Reds, I would fill the oceans all over the world with radioactive fish. It would be so easy to do!"[144] Neither the Japanese nor most Americans accepted Strauss's explanation, and the United States eventually issued a formal apology to Japan and paid the Japanese $2 million in compensation. Nevertheless, the United States

Nuclear Warhead Stockpiles, 1945-1995						
	1945	1955	1965	1975	1985	1995
UNITED STATES	6	3,057	31,265	26,675	22,941	14,766
SOVIET UNION	0	200	6,129	19,443	39,197	27,000
BRITAIN	0	10	310	350	300	300
FRANCE	0	0	32	188	360	485
CHINA	0	0	5	185	425	425

Note: Figures are estimates and include strategic and nonstrategic warheads scheduled to be dismantled.

continued to expand its nuclear arsenal, prompting a variety of calls for an end to nuclear weapons.

Einstein joined forces with another noted scientist, Albert Schweitzer, in calling for an end to nuclear bomb testing. In 1955 Einstein wrote that should a war erupt between the United States and Soviet Union, "mankind is doomed."[145] He added:

Despite this knowledge, statesmen in responsible positions on both sides continue to employ the well-known technique of seeking to intimidate and demoralize the opponent by marshaling superior military strength. They do so even though such a policy entails the risk of war and doom. Not one statesman in a position of responsibility has dared to pursue the only course that holds out any promise of peace, the course of supranational security, since for a statesman to follow such a course would be tantamount to political suicide. Political passions, once they have been fanned into flame, exact their victims.[146]

Eventually, some politicians did become involved in calling for at least a ban on some kinds of nuclear bomb testing. During the 1956 presidential campaign, candidate Adlai Stevenson called for a ban on testing the bombs in the atmosphere.

Many Americans soon followed suit, giving birth to a ban-the-bomb movement in the 1950s and 1960s. A number of Americans began to protest the testing and, in time, the very existence of nuclear weapons. They even protested the futility of seeking shelter in the event of a nuclear war. A mother and daughter boycotting an air-raid drill in New York City, for example, carried signs reading, respectively, "There is no shelter in nuclear war" and "I want to grow up."[147]

SANE Versus MAD

Citizens groups whose goal was global peace began to spring up throughout the country during the 1950s. One such group, SANE—A Citizens' Organization for a SANE World, began a high-profile advertising campaign calling on the United States and Soviet Union to stop developing and testing nuclear weapons. SANE chose its name to distinguish itself from the bedrock principle on which the nation's nuclear weapons strategy was built—mutual assured destruction, or MAD. SANE enlisted the support of the well-known pediatrician Benjamin Spock, author of *Baby and Child Care*. In addition to speaking for the group, Spock also appeared in full-page ads for SANE, including one in which, with a look of concern on his face, he gazes at a little girl. The caption read, "Dr. Spock is worried."[148] Partially as a result of the advertising campaign, more than twenty-four thousand Americans joined SANE. Another large citizens group to emerge during this time was launched by the philosopher Bertrand Russell. His group, the Campaign for Nuclear Disar-

Groups such as SANE emerged to protest the continuation of nuclear testing.

mament, argued that the United States should shed its nuclear arsenal, even if the Soviet Union kept its weapons. The Campaign for Nuclear Disarmament quickly became the largest in the world to lobby for unilateral disarmament. Other antinuclear groups were formed in the 1960s, including the Council for a Livable World, which was established by a nuclear physicist to warn about the dangers of nuclear war. One group established in the 1960s to protest the Vietnam War, Clergy and Laity Concerned about the War in Vietnam, later changed its name to Clergy and Laity Concerned and its focus to the menace of nuclear weapons.

The ban-the-bomb movement gained momentum when scientists discovered that fallout from aboveground nuclear tests was entering the food chain, and hence, Americans. In 1958 the Committee for Nuclear Information at Washington University in St. Louis collected tens of thousands of baby teeth. Scientists discovered strontium 90, a component of fallout, in the teeth and concluded that the fallout was landing on grass that was eaten by cows, then passed by them through their milk and meat into humans.

Not all Americans protested nuclear weapons by joining public interest groups. Some protested in song. Tom Lehrer, a

Cuban Missile Crisis

The events of October 1962 would help to galvanize opposition to nuclear weapons, uniting a substantial number of Americans behind the ban-the-bomb movement. What stirred the growing antinuclear sentiment was an event that came to be known as the Cuban missile crisis.

On October 15, 1962, U.S. spy planes snapped pictures that would bring the world to the very brink of nuclear war. The photographs revealed construction in Cuba of eight missile launchpads. President John F. Kennedy immediately ordered a blockade of Cuba, then explained to Americans that the action was necessary because nuclear weapons, if allowed to be positioned in Cuba, would have the capability of destroying a number of U.S. cities.

The United States and Soviet Union played a high-stakes game of chicken for the next thirteen days. Peter Jennings and Todd Brewster recalled those tense days in *The Century*:

> From the Vatican, Pope John XXIII pleaded with the two leaders to consider their obligations not only to the interests of their respective states but to humanity, which hung in the balance. The *Los Angeles Times*

reported that students at local high schools were breaking down in class and sobbing, "I don't want to die." But the preparations for war continued. American [intercontinental ballistic missiles] at silo bases across the West were loaded and cocked for delivery; fleets of American Polaris submarines, armed with nuclear missiles, were set on an approach to Soviet waters. The nation's air force was put on DEFCON2 (an acronym standing for Defense Condition 2, DEFCON1 being a state of war), the highest alert in the post–World War II era, while sixteen navy destroyers and three cruise ships formed a five-hundred-mile arc interrupting access to the east coast of Cuba. Still, twenty-five Soviet merchant ships headed there stayed on course. Kennedy was pushing forward plans for an air attack on Cuba, followed by an invasion.

Tensions eventually subsided, the Soviets dropped plans to install missiles in Cuba, and the United States eased off its war preparations. But for two weeks in October, the entire world wondered whether the world's final war was at hand.

---

mathematician and songwriter, took sharp aim at U.S. nuclear policy. In a popular 1953 album, "The Wild West Is Where I Want to Be," he sang:

> Along the trail you'll find me lopin'
> Where the spaces are wide open,
> In the land of the old A.E.C. [Atomic
>   Energy Commission]
> Where the scenery's attractive,
> And the air is radioactive,
> Oh, the wild west is where I want to be.

> 'Mid the sagebrush and the
>   cactus
> I'll watch the fellers practice
> Droppin' bombs through the clean
>   desert breeze.
> I'll have on my sombrero,
> And of course I'll wear a pair o'
> Levis over my lead B.V.D.'s [a brand
>   of underwear][149]

Six years later, Lehrer in "We Will All Go Together When We Go," pointed to the consequence of any use of nuclear weapons. He sang:

And we will all go together when we go,
Ev'ry Hottentot and ev'ry Eskimo
When the air becomes uranious,
We will all go simultaneous,
Yes, we will all go together
When we all go together,
Yes, we all will go together when
    we go.[150]

"A Shaft of Light"

The widespread protests would eventually bear fruit when the United States and Soviet Union agreed in 1958 to an informal moratorium on aboveground nuclear testing. However, negotiations to make the ban permanent were snagged. Eventually, as tensions between the two nations escalated, Soviet premier Nikita Khrushchev on August 30, 1961, announced the Soviets would conduct atmospheric tests every two days for two months. Among the blasts was a thirty-megaton bomb and a fifty-megaton bomb—two thousand five hundred times more powerful than the Hiroshima atom bomb. Although President Kennedy decided to hold off on further U.S. tests until April 1962, the Soviet tests troubled him and outraged groups such as SANE.

On June 10, 1963, Kennedy delivered a speech in which he denounced communism but expressed respect for the Soviet people. Echoing the words of anti-

nuclear protesters, he went on to note that, on "this small planet, we all breathe the same air. We all cherish our children's future. And we are all mortal."[151] Because of the increasingly deadly nature of nuclear weapons, he said that peace was "the necessary rational end of rational men," adding that the United States would not explode any more nuclear weapons aboveground "so long as other states do not do so."[152] The speech had the desired result, and on July 25, 1963, the United States and Soviet Union agreed to ban all tests of nuclear weapons in the atmosphere, outer space, and under water. Underground tests, however, were not banned and ultimately increased. Nevertheless, the agreement relieved Kennedy, who likened the development to "a shaft of light cut into the darkness."[153]

The agreement also cheered antinuclear Americans, though they wondered whether the light Kennedy spoke of represented the proverbial end of the tunnel. For many years it appeared that it was not, as the United States and Soviet Union continued developing nuclear weapons and plans to use them. The ban-the-bomb movement, however, receded in popularity as many Americans turned to protesting the Vietnam War and social injustice. However, governmental efforts to limit nuclear weapons would continue nonetheless. In late May 1972, under President Richard M. Nixon, the two countries finally wrapped up negotiations on Strategic Arms Limitation Talks, or SALT, that

President Kennedy (center, left) and Soviet Premier Nikita Khrushchev (center, right) met to discuss the future of nuclear testing.

had been under way for three years. Although the resulting treaty was less effective than initially believed, it opened up a new atmosphere in relations between the two countries. That new flavor was dubbed "détente," and referred to the easing of the open hostility between the two nuclear powers. Under détente, the two countries negotiated with each other instead of seeking confrontations, a cooperative spirit that also led to agreements on such issues as the environment, space, and public health. Moreover, the arms talks continued. In 1974, under President Gerald R. Ford's leadership, the coun-

tries agreed to limit the number of nuclear weapons carriers—missiles, submarines, and planes—to two thousand four hundred. However, the United States Senate refused to ratify the agreement, and the two countries continued their uneasy, adversarial relationship.

Reagan Policies Revitalize Movement

Ford was succeeded in office by Jimmy Carter, who fully supported a continuation of the SALT process. The resulting negotiations, which would have imposed important new restrictions on nuclear weapons, fell apart, however, when the Soviet Union invaded Afghanistan. These renewed tensions prompted Carter to sign Presidential Directive-59 before he left office, which committed the nation to fight a prolonged nuclear war with the Soviets.

When Ronald W. Reagan took over the presidency in 1981, he expanded on Carter's directive. In National Security Directive 13, Reagan stated that "should deterrence fail and strategic nuclear war with the U.S.S.R. occur, the United States must prevail and be able to force the Soviet Union to seek earliest termination of hostilities favorable to the United States."[154] Whereas Carter committed the nation to fighting a prolonged nuclear war, Reagan committed the nation to winning it. To back up his pledge, Reagan launched an unprecedented military buildup costing $1.5 trillion over five years. To many Americans, it seemed that the United States was closer than ever to nuclear holocaust.

Reagan's military buildup revitalized the ban-the-bomb movement. For example, the Union of Concerned Scientists, which had opposed nuclear power in the 1970s, became a harsh critic of nuclear weapons in the 1980s. Local groups also formed to protest nuclear weaponry. For example, a group calling itself the Ground Zero Center for Nonviolent Action was established in Poulsbo, Washington, near a naval base that was home to submarines armed with nuclear missiles. Physicians for Social Responsibility, which was established during the 1960s to protest nuclear power, was revitalized and spoke out against nuclear weapons. While

it began the 1980s with only a handful of members, membership shot up to 30,000 with 180 chapters throughout the United States by 1983.

Children Speak Out

Physicians for Social Responsibility president Helen Caldicott, an Australian pediatrician, traveled across the United States to give lectures on the medical implications of nuclear war. At the same time, the Union of Concerned Scientists began to hold a number of meetings at colleges across the country, examining the threat of nuclear war and ways of avoiding one. Other groups such as the United Campuses to Prevent Nuclear War and Lawyers Alliance for Nuclear Arms Control also planned antinuclear meetings on college campuses as ever-increasing numbers of Americans began to speak out against the weapons.

Even children joined their voices to the growing antinuclear chorus. Some sent moving letters to Reagan in bewildered protest. One such letter read:

President Reagan,

Why do you won't [sic] to kill harmless children? Why do you make new bombs? Why do you won't [sic] to destory [sic] the only world, why?

Singed [sic] Brian[155]

Reagan was not deaf to public concerns. Realizing that public anxiety was

Three Mile Island

Although many Americans were disturbed by the nation's reliance on nuclear weapons during the Cold War, some saw hope in the rise of nuclear power plants that held out the promise that the United States could be freed from its dependence on fossil fuels. Others, however, worried that an accident at such a power plant could have results every bit as terrible as a nuclear war.

The nation came perilously close to finding out on March 28, 1979, when a broken valve allowed coolant to drain from the Three Mile Island nuclear reactor, perched along the Susquehanna River in Pennsylvania Dutch country. Without the coolant, exposed fuel rods began to melt in temperatures that rose to more than five thousand degrees. An emergency evacuation was ordered, and a catastrophe was averted only when the molten material stopped on the reactor floor. Had it gone through the floor, a meltdown—vast quantities of highly toxic radioactivity—would have been released into the atmosphere. As it was, small amounts of radioactive material did escape. Reactor officials said the levels were insignificant, but others were not so sure. About the only thing everyone could agree on was that it could have been much worse.

Three Mile Island.

reaching extreme levels, Reagan told Americans he believed the nation's technological know-how would allow the United States to create a space-based defensive system that could shoot down Soviet missiles before they hit the United States. Reagan called the plan the Strategic Defense Initiative, but the press quickly labeled the plan Star Wars, because it sounded like fantastic science fiction. Although the plan may have eased some domestic fears temporarily, they only ratcheted up concern in Moscow, where leaders believed such a technology would allow the United States to strike the Soviet Union with impunity.

Some Nuclear Missiles Destroyed

The arms race continued, and public fears were further fueled by respected scientists who postulated that, even if people survived nuclear blasts and the resulting radiation, all life on the planet would likely perish from a nuclear winter, a phenomenon caused by the vast amounts of smoke and debris that would be released into the atmosphere by multiple nuclear explosions. Under the nuclear winter theory, these clouds would block out the sun, and Earth would rapidly become uninhabitable.

The ban-the-bomb movement achieved a breakthrough when Mikhail Gorbachev became leader of the Soviet Union. A realist, Gorbachev saw how the costly and expanding arms race had bankrupted his nation. He took steps to improve political freedom within the country and to make the economy less reliant on the government. For his part, Reagan saw in Gorbachev an opportunity. The two men met a number of times, and at Reykjavík, Iceland, during a two-day conference in which Reagan and Gorbachev were together for nearly ten hours of negotiations, they had an enormous breakthrough. The leaders agreed to cut nuclear forces in half, and then excitedly discussed the possibility of

completely dismantling nuclear forces. Reagan said, "I have a picture that after ten years you and I come to Iceland and bring the last two missiles in the world and have the biggest damn celebration of it!"[156] However, Gorbachev wanted Reagan to shelve the Strategic Defense Initiative, which Reagan was unwilling to do. The president offered to share the defensive system with the Soviets, but in the end, the deal collapsed.

In February 1987, however, Gorbachev relented, saying he would be willing to destroy some nuclear weapons. Reagan and Gorbachev on December 8, 1987, agreed to destroy 859 American missiles and 1,836 Soviet missiles located

Mikhail Gorbachev (left) met on several occasions with President Ronald Reagan (right) to discuss nuclear armaments of their respective countries.

in Europe and Asia. It was the first-ever agreement to destroy nuclear weapons and would not be the last. Gorbachev in 1991 signed a Strategic Arms Reduction Talks with President George Herbert Walker Bush that called for the destruction of a significant number of longer-range nuclear weapons.

"A Path Where No Man Thought"

The nuclear age began with fear and guilt, and those two emotions remained high throughout the duration of the Cold War. But even after the Cold War concluded, many Americans could not help but shudder at the awesome destructive power contained in the nuclear weapons that both the United States and Russia still held. Although a public outcry—and economic considerations—ultimately brought about an end to the arms race, the world at Cold War's end appeared in as precarious a position as it did when scientists first unleashed the power of the atom. As scientists Carl Sagan and Richard Turco put it, however, the fear that accompanied the end of the Cold War also carried with it hope. They wrote:

> Never before in human history has there been such a degree of shared vulnerability. Every nation now has an urgent stake in the activities of its fellow nations. This is most true—because here the danger is greatest—on the question of nuclear weapons. Nuclear winter has alerted us to our common peril and our mutual dependence. It reaffirms an ancient truth: When we kill our brother, we kill ourselves.

> We have entered a most promising time—not just because the walls are tumbling down, not just because money and scientific talent long devoted to the military will now become available for urgent civilian concerns, but also because we finally are becoming aware of our unsuspected—indeed, awesome—powers over the environment that sustains us. Like the assault on the protective ozone layer and global greenhouse warming, nuclear winter is a looming planetwide catastrophe that is within our power to avert. It teaches us the need for foresight and wisdom as we haltingly negotiate our way out of technological adolescence.

> From the halls of high Olympus, where strange dooms are stored for humans, there is reason to hope that, in our time also, there is a way out—a path where no man thought.[157]

★ Notes ★

Introduction: "An Iron Curtain Has Descended"

1. Quoted in Allan M. Winkler, *The Cold War: A History in Documents.* Oxford: Oxford University Press, 2000, p. 22.

Chapter 1: Fear and Prosperity

2. Henry Luce in "The American Century," in John K. Jessup, ed., *The Ideas of Henry Luce.* New York: Atheneum, 1969, p. 116.
3. Quoted in John Sharnik, *Inside the Cold War: An Oral History.* New York: Arbor House, 1987, p. 339.
4. Quoted in Peter Jennings and Todd Brewster, *The Century.* New York: Doubleday, 1998, p. 286.
5. Quoted in Jennings and Brewster, *The Century,* p. 328.
6. Depicted in photograph in Jennings and Brewster, *The Century,* p. 289.
7. Quoted in Jennings and Brewster, *The Century,* p. 284.
8. Quoted in Winkler, *The Cold War,* p. 33.
9. Quoted in Editors of Time-Life Books, *This Fabulous Century: 1950–1960.* Alexandria, VA: Time-Life Books, 1985, p. 26.
10. Quoted in Jennings and Brewster, *The Century,* p. 292.
11. Ann Douglas in "An Age of Boom and Belief," in Richard B. Stolley, ed., *Life: Our Century in Pictures.* Boston: Bullfinch, 1999, p. 222.
12. Quoted in Editors of Time-Life Books, *This Fabulous Century: 1950–1960,* p. 27.
13. Quoted in Editors of Time-Life Books, *The American Dream: the 50s.* Alexandria, VA: Time-Life Books, 1998, p. 86.
14. Quoted in Jennings and Brewster, *The Century,* p. 292.
15. Quoted in Editors of Time-Life Books, *The American Dream,* p. 86.
16. Quoted in Editors of Time-Life Books, *The American Dream,* p. 88.
17. Quoted in Editors of Time-Life Books, *This Fabulous Century: 1950–1960,* p. 25.
18. John Steinbeck, *Travels with Charley in Search of America.* New York: Bantam Books, 1977, p. 129.
19. Quoted in Jennings and Brewster, *The Century,* p. 286.
20. Quoted in Karal Ann Marling, *As Seen on TV: The Visual Culture of Everyday Life in the 1950s.* Cambridge, MA: Harvard University Press, 1994, p. 51.

21. Quoted in Marling, *As Seen on TV,* p. 58.
22. Quoted in Marling, *As Seen on TV,* pp. 59–60.
23. Quoted in Marling, *As Seen on TV,* p. 62.
24. Quoted in Marling, *As Seen on TV,* p. 64.

Chapter 2: The Spies Among U.S.

25. Quoted in Allen Weinstein, *Perjury: The Hiss-Chambers Case.* New York: Alfred A. Knopf, 1978, p. 4.
26. Quoted in Don Lawson, *The KGB: The True Story of Russia's Spy Network!* New York: Julian Messner, 1984, p. 138.
27. Quoted in Lawson, *The KGB,* p. 134.
28. Quoted in Sam Tanenhaus, *Whittaker Chambers: A Biography.* New York: Random House, 1997, p. 220.
29. Quoted in Tanenhaus, *Whittaker Chambers,* p. 220.
30. Quoted in Weinstein, *Perjury,* p. 5.
31. Quoted in Tanenhaus, *Whittaker Chambers,* p. 219.
32. Quoted in Tanenhaus, *Whittaker Chambers,* p. 221.
33. Quoted in Tanenhaus, *Whittaker Chambers,* p. 217.
34. Quoted in Tanenhaus, *Whittaker Chambers,* p. 221.
35. Quoted in Weinstein, *Perjury,* p. 6.
36. Quoted in Tanenhaus, *Whittaker Chambers,* p. 222.
37. Quoted in Weinstein, *Perjury,* p. 8.
38. Quoted in Lawson, *The KGB,* p. 143.
39. Quoted in Walter Schneir and Miriam Schneir, *Invitation to an Inquest.* Garden City, NY: Doubleday, 1965, p. 53.
40. Quoted in Schneir and Schneir, *Invitation,* p. 53.
41. Quoted in Schneir and Schneir, *Invitation,* p. 53.
42. Quoted in Lawson, *The KGB,* p. 130.
43. Quoted in Schneir and Schneir, *Invitation,* p. 169.
44. Quoted in Schneir and Schneir, *Invitation,* p. 170.
45. Quoted in Schneir and Schneir, *Invitation,* p. 170.
46. Quoted in Schneir and Schneir, *Invitation,* p. 171.
47. Quoted in Lawson, *The KGB,* p. 131.
48. Quoted in Lawson, *The KGB,* p. 131.
49. Quoted in Harold Evans, *The American Century.* New York: Alfred A. Knopf, 1998, p. 443.

Chapter 3: McCarthyism

50. Quoted in Editors of Time-Life Books, *The American Dream,* p. 80.
51. Quoted in Editors of Time-Life Books, *The American Dream,* p. 80.
52. Quoted in Evans, *The American Century,* p. 445.
53. Quoted in Editors of Time-Life Books, *The American Dream,* p. 80.
54. Quoted in Winkler, *The Cold War,* p. 62.
55. Quoted in Evans, *The American Century,* p. 446.

56. Quoted in Robert Meeropol and Michael Meeropol, *We Are Your Sons: The Legacy of Ethel and Julius Rosenberg.* Urbana: University of Illinois Press, 1986, p. 349.

57. Quoted in Meeropol and Meeropol, *We Are Your Sons,* p. 349.

58. Quoted in Meeropol and Meeropol, *We Are Your Sons,* p. 349.

59. Quoted in Meeropol and Meeropol, *We Are Your Sons,* p. 349.

60. Quoted in Evans, *The American Century,* p. 444.

61. Quoted in Winkler, *The Cold War,* p. 68.

62. Quoted in Winkler, *The Cold War,* p. 68.

63. Quoted in Winkler, *The Cold War,* p. 67.

64. Quoted in Winkler, *The Cold War,* p. 68.

65. Quoted in Winkler, *The Cold War,* p. 68.

66. Quoted in Winkler, *The Cold War,* p. 69.

67. Quoted in Winkler, *The Cold War,* p. 69.

68. Quoted in Ellen Schrecker, *Many Are the Crimes: McCarthyism in America.* Boston: Little, Brown, 1998, p. 184.

69. Quoted in Schrecker, *Many Are the Crimes,* p. 184.

70. Quoted in Schrecker, *Many Are the Crimes,* p. 184.

71. Quoted in Schrecker, *Many Are the Crimes,* p. 185.

72. Quoted in Elder Witt, ed., *Congressional Quarterly's Guide to the U.S. Supreme Court.* Washington, DC: Congressional Quarterly, 1979, p. 511.

73. Quoted in Winkler, *The Cold War,* p. 46.

74. Quoted in Winkler, *The Cold War,* p. 48.

75. Quoted in Winkler, *The Cold War,* p. 48.

76. Quoted in Winkler, *The Cold War,* p. 50.

Chapter 4: The Space Race

77. Quoted in Paul Dickson, *Sputnik: The Shock of the Century,* New York: Walker, 2001, p. 11.

78. Quoted in Dickson, *Sputnik,* p. 11.

79. Quoted in Dickson, *Sputnik,* p. 9.

80. Quoted in Dickson, *Sputnik,* p. 17.

81. Quoted in Dickson, *Sputnik,* p. 13.

82. Quoted in Dickson, *Sputnik,* p. 18.

83. Quoted in T.A. Heppenheimer, *Countdown: A History of Space Flight.* New York: John Wiley & Sons, 1997, p. 124.

84. Quoted in Heppenheimer, *Countdown,* p. 124.

85. Quoted in Dickson, *Sputnik,* p. 19.

86. Quoted in Dickson, *Sputnik,* p. 22.

87. Quoted in Dickson, *Sputnik,* p. 22.

88. Quoted in Heppenheimer, *Countdown,* p. 124.

89. Quoted in Writers and Editors of The Associated Press, *Footprints on the Moon.* New York: Associated Press, 1969, p. 3.

90. Quoted in Heppenheimer, *Countdown*, p. 124.

91. Quoted in Dickson, *Sputnik*, pp. 22–23.

92. Quoted in Dickson, *Sputnik*, p. 23.

93. Quoted in Heppenheimer, *Countdown*, p. 124.

94. Quoted in Editors of Time-Life Books, *The American Dream*, p. 92.

95. Quoted in Editors of Time-Life Books, *The American Dream*, p. 92.

96. Quoted in Heppenheimer, *Countdown*, p. 125.

97. Quoted in Heppenheimer, *Countdown*, p. 125.

98. Quoted in Heppenheimer, *Countdown*, p. 126.

99. Quoted in Sharnik, *Inside the Cold War*, p. 105.

100. Quoted in David Halberstam, *The Fifties*. New York: Villard Books, 1993, p. 627.

101. Quoted in Heppenheimer, *Countdown*, p. 127.

102. Quoted in Heppenheimer, *Countdown*, p. 128.

103. Quoted in Heppenheimer, *Countdown*, p. 129.

104. Quoted in Dickson, *Sputnik*, p. 175.

105. Quoted in Writers and Editors of The Associated Press, *Footprints*, p. 5.

106. Quoted in Writers and Editors of The Associated Press, *Footprints*, p. 5.

107. Quoted in Writers and Editors of The Associated Press, *Footprints*, p. 6.

108. Quoted in Writers and Editors of The Associated Press, *Footprints*, p. 15.

109. Quoted in Editors of Time-Life Books, *This Fabulous Century: 1960–1970*. Alexandria, VA: Time-Life Books, 1985, p. 269.

110. Quoted in Editors of Time-Life Books, *This Fabulous Century: 1960–1970*, p. 279.

111. Quoted in Editors of Time-Life Books, *This Fabulous Century: 1960–1970*, p. 279.

112. Quoted in Editors of Time-Life Books, *This Fabulous Century: 1960–1970*, p. 280.

113. Quoted in Editors of Time-Life Books, *This Fabulous Century: 1960–1970*, p. 280.

114. Quoted in Writers and Editors of The Associated Press, *Footprints*, p. 210.

115. Quoted in Dickson, *Sputnik*, p. 241.

Chapter 5: The Military-Industrial Complex

116. William Greider, *Fortress America: The American Military and the Consequences of Peace*. New York: Public Affairs, 1998, p. xvi.

117. Quoted in Tim Weiner, *Blank Check: The Pentagon's Black Budget*. New York: Warner Books, 1990, p. 25.

118. Quoted in Weiner, *Blank Check*, p. 25.

119. Quoted in Weiner, *Blank Check*, p. 27.

120. Quoted in Weiner, *Blank Check*, p. 27.

121. Quoted in Editors of Time-Life Books, *The American Dream*, p. 77.

122. Quoted in Winkler, *The Cold War*, p. 37.
123. Quoted in Winkler, *The Cold War*, p. 37.
124. Quoted in Winkler, *The Cold War*, p. 38.
125. Quoted in Winkler, *The Cold War*, p. 38.
126. Quoted in Weiner, *Blank Check*, p. 30.
127. Quoted in Weiner, *Blank Check*, p. 32.
128. Quoted in Weiner, *Blank Check*, p. 32.
129. Quoted in Weiner, *Blank Check*, p. 33.
130. Quoted in Winkler, *The Cold War*, p. 81.
131. Quoted in Weiner, *Blank Check*, p. 33.
132. Quoted in Weiner, *Blank Check*, p. 36.
133. Quoted in Winkler, *The Cold War*, p. 84.
134. Quoted in Winkler, *The Cold War*, p. 84.
135. Quoted in Winkler, *The Cold War*, p. 84.
136. Quoted in Winkler, *The Cold War*, pp. 84–85.
137. Quoted in Marling, *As Seen on TV*, p. 252.
138. Quoted in Marling, *As Seen on TV*, p. 252.
139. Quoted in Marling, *As Seen on TV*, p. 252.

Chapter 6: "Mankind Is Doomed"

140. Quoted in Halberstam, *The Fifties*, p. 34.
141. Quoted in Judith Bentley, *The Nuclear Freeze Movement*. New York: Franklin Watts, 1984, p. 15.
142. Quoted in Halberstam, *The Fifties*, p. 35.
143. Quoted in Winkler, *The Cold War*, p. 81.
144. Quoted in Editors of Time-Life Books, *This Fabulous Century: 1950–1960*, p. 31.
145. Quoted in Carl Sagan and Richard Turco, *A Path Where No Man Thought: Nuclear Winter and the End of the Arms Race*. New York: Random House, 1990, p. 71.
146. Quoted in Sagan and Turco, *A Path Where No Man Thought*, p. 300.
147. Quoted in Editors of Time-Life Books, *The American Dream*, p. 90.
148. Depicted in a photograph in Winkler, *The Cold War*, p. 102.
149. Quoted in Winkler, *The Cold War*, p. 82.
150. Quoted in Winkler, *The Cold War*, p. 82.
151. Quoted in Evans, *The American Century*, p. 497.
152. Quoted in Evans, *The American Century*, p. 497.
153. Quoted in Evans, *The American Century*, p. 497.
154. Quoted in Winkler, *The Cold War*, p. 140.
155. Reproduced in Winkler, *The Cold War*, p. 141.
156. Quoted in Evans, *The American Century*, p. 646.
157. Quoted in Sagan and Turco, *A Path Where No Man Thought*, pp. 300–301.

★ Chronology of Events ★

1945

26 July: As World War II continues in the Pacific, the United States tests an atomic bomb in the New Mexico desert.

6 August: United States drops atomic bomb on Hiroshima, Japan.

9 August: United States drops atomic bomb on Nagasaki, Japan.

14 August: Japan surrenders.

1946

5 March: Former British prime minister Winston Churchill delivers famous "Iron Curtain" speech in Fulton, Missouri, warning that the Soviet Union is intent on spreading its Communist ideology worldwide.

1947

27 October: Ring Lardner Jr., one of the Hollywood Ten, testifies before the House Un-American Activities Committee as part of the panel's investigation into Communist infiltration of the motion picture industry.

1948

3 August: Time magazine writer and editor Whittaker Chambers tells Congress that respected former State Department official Alger Hiss is a Communist.

15 December: A grand jury indicts Hiss for perjury.

1949

8 July: Hiss perjury trial ends in a hung jury.

3 September: Air force reconnaissance plane detects signs of atomic testing by the Soviet Union.

1950

21 January: Second Hiss perjury trial concludes; Hiss convicted.

3 February: Former Manhattan Project physicist Klaus Fuchs confesses to being a Soviet spy.

9 February: Senator Joseph McCarthy alleges in a speech that more than two hundred State Department employees are members of the Communist Party.

7 April: President Harry S. Truman's National Security Council commits the United States to a massive military buildup to thwart Soviet expansionism.

17 July: Julius Rosenberg arrested on charges that he was a leader of a Soviet spy ring that stole U.S. atom bomb secrets.

11 August: Ethel Rosenberg, Julius Rosenberg's wife, also arrested for espionage.

1952

1 November: United States tests world's first hydrogen bomb.

1953

19 June: Julius and Ethel Rosenberg are executed for conspiring to spy against the United States.

12 August: Soviets test their first hydrogen bomb.

1954

9 June: Army-McCarthy hearings come to a head when lawyer Joseph Welch challenges McCarthy; senator's popularity slides.

2 December: Senate condemns McCarthy.

1957

4 October: Soviet Union launches *Sputnik*, first man-made Earth satellite.

6 December: U.S. Navy's *Vanguard*, expected to be first U.S. Earth satellite, explodes on the launchpad.

1958

31 January: An army rocket launches first U.S. satellite into space.

17 March: Navy gets *Vanguard* satellite into orbit.

1 October: National Aeronautics and Space Administration (NASA) officially opens.

1961

17 January: President Dwight D. Eisenhower's farewell address warns of the dangers of a growing "military-industrial complex."

12 April: Soviet cosmonaut Yuri Gagarin becomes first person to travel in space.

5 May: Alan Shepard becomes first American to travel in space.

25 May: President John F. Kennedy commits nation to being first to land a man on the moon and bring him home safely.

1962

15 October: U.S. spy plane discovers Soviets are installing nuclear weapon launch sites in Cuba.

28 October: Soviets agree to remove weapons from Cuba.

1963

25 July: United States and Soviet Union agree to end all nuclear weapons tests in the Earth's atmosphere, under water, and in outer space; underground nuclear tests continue.

1969

20 July: *Apollo 11* lands on moon.

1972

26 May: United States and Soviet Union successfully conclude strategic arms limitation talks (SALT), creating a new atmosphere of trust between the two countries.

1979

18 July: President Jimmy Carter and Soviet leader Leonid Brezhnev sign SALT II, another arms control treaty; however, the Senate does not ratify the document.

1986

11–12 October: President Ronald Reagan and Soviet leader Mikhail Gorbachev meet in Iceland and agree to drastic cuts in nuclear weapons. The deal snags on Reagan's refusal to shelve plans for a missile defense system.

1987

8 December: United States and Soviet Union agree to dismantle nuclear weapons in Asia and Europe.

1989

November: East German Communist leader opens East Germany's borders; thousands of Germans destroy the twenty-eight-mile-long Berlin Wall.

1992

28 January: President George Bush in his State of the Union address announces that the Cold War is over and that the United States is victorious.

★ For Further Reading ★

Simon Adams, *Visual Timeline of the 20th Century*. New York: DK Publishing, 1996. A colorful and richly illustrated history of the twentieth century, including the Cold War between the United States and Soviet Union.

Trevor Cairns, *The Twentieth Century*. Minneapolis: Lerner Publications, 1984. Examines significant events of the century, including Cold War tensions.

Leila Merrell Foster, *The Story of the Cold War*. Chicago: Childrens Press, 1990. A broad look at the prolonged period of antagonism between the United States and Soviet Union.

Susan Dudley Gold, *Arms Control*. New York: Twenty-First Century Books, 1997. Examines the role of treaties in promoting world peace and provides an overview of attempts to control the arms race through treaties.

Nigel Hawkes, *Nuclear Arms Race*. New York: Gloucester Press, 1986. Provides a broad overview of the complexity of the world's nuclear arms stockpiles and nations' attempts at keeping them under control.

Warren A. James, *Cold War: The American Crusade Against World Communism, 1945–1991*. New York: Lothrop, Lee & Shepard Books, 1996. Provides an intriguing overview of the United States' Cold War with the Soviet Union.

Michael G. Kort, *The Cold War*. Brookfield, CT: Millbrook, 1994. Provides an overview of the long ideological conflict between the Communist world and Western democracies that took root following World War II and flourished until communism collapsed in Europe in the 1990s.

Melinda Moore and Laurie Olsen, *Our Future at Stake: A Teenager's Guide to Stopping the Nuclear Arms Race*. Philadelphia: New Society, 1985. A broad overview of the escalating arms race along with practical tips for becoming involved in the public debate over nuclear weapons.

Victoria Sherrow, *Joseph McCarthy and the Cold War*. Woodbridge, CT: Blackbirch, 1999. A biography of the Wisconsin senator who rose from obscurity with his campaign to root out what he perceived as a large number of Communists in the U.S. government.

☆ Works Consulted ☆

Judith Bentley, *The Nuclear Freeze Movement*. New York: Franklin Watts, 1984. Offers an intriguing examination of grassroots efforts to stem the spread and use of nuclear weapons.

Seweryn Bialer and Michael Mandelbaum, *The Global Rivals: The Forty-Year Contest for Supremacy*. New York: Alfred A. Knopf, 1988. A reasoned hypothesis of the challenges and opportunities facing the United States and Soviet Union in the years to come, written prior to the collapse of the Soviet Union.

Piers Brendon, *Ike: His Life & Times*. New York: Harper and Row, 1986. An insightful biography of Dwight D. Eisenhower.

Christopher Brookeman, *American Culture and Society Since the 1930s*. New York: Schocken Books, 1984. A thorough though somewhat esoteric examination of the social and intellectual climate of post–World War II America.

E.H. Cookridge, *Spy Trade*. New York: Walker, 1971. Examines a unique aspect of the Cold War, the bartering done by the United States and USSR for captured spies.

Charles Dickens, *A Tale of Two Cities*. New York: Book-of-the-Month Club, 1998. A classic novel set during the French Revolution.

Paul Dickson, *Sputnik: The Shock of the Century*. New York: Walker, 2001. A gripping account of the developments that both led to and followed the Soviet Union's successful *Sputnik* launch.

Editors of Time-Life Books, *The American Dream: The 50s*. Alexandria, VA: Time-Life Books, 1998. A lavishly illustrated and informative work that outlines the contradictions of a rich period in American history.

———, *This Fabulous Century: 1950–1960*. Alexandria, VA: Time-Life Books, 1985. A broad look at a decade of fear and optimism.

———, *This Fabulous Century: 1960–1970*. Alexandria, VA: Time-Life Books, 1985. A fascinating examination of a turbulent decade.

Harold Evans, *The American Century*. New York: Alfred A. Knopf, 1998. A richly illustrated and intriguing overview of the twentieth century in the United States.

William Bragg Ewald Jr., *Who Killed Joe McCarthy?* New York: Simon & Schuster, 1984. An intriguing behind-the-scenes look at McCarthy's intemperate crusade against communism.

George Feifer, *Red Files: Secrets from the Russian Archives.* New York: TV Books, 2000. A unique and intriguing look at the Cold War, supplemented with information from once-secret Soviet documents.

A. Ernest Fitzgerald, *The High Priests of Waste.* New York: W.W. Norton, 1972. An inside look at bureaucratic incompetence within the military-industrial complex that resulted in the U.S. military's purchase of inferior goods at inflated costs.

John Lewis Gaddis, *The United States and the End of the Cold War: Implications, Reconsiderations, Provocations.* New York: Oxford University Press, 1992. A thoughtful examination of how the Cold War was won, and what that victory means for the future.

William Greider, *Fortress America: The American Military and the Consequences of Peace.* New York: Public Affairs, 1998. A startling examination of the U.S. military in the early post–Cold War period.

David Halberstam, *The Fifties.* New York: Villard Books, 1993. A sweeping and engaging examination of the 1950s, with telling detail and insight.

Edward H. Harvey Jr., ed., *Our Glorious Century.* Pleasantville, NY: Reader's Digest Association, 1994. A broad and intriguing examination of the main events and cultural landscape of the United States during the twentieth century.

T.A. Heppenheimer, *Countdown: A History of Space Flight.* New York: John Wiley & Sons, 1997. A unique, behind-the-scenes look at the U.S. and Soviet space programs, as well as a general overview of man's quest to explore space.

Arthur Herman, *Joseph McCarthy: Reexamining the Life and Legacy of America's Most Hated Senator.* New York: Free Press, 2000. A balanced look at the Wisconsin senator whose response to the "red scare" instilled fear and destroyed reputations.

Tony Hiss, *The View from Alger's Window: A Son's Memoir.* New York: Alfred A. Knopf, 1999. A moving memoir written by Alger Hiss's son, including many previously unpublished letters Alger Hiss wrote his son from prison.

Peter Jennings and Todd Brewster, *The Century.* New York: Doubleday, 1998. A comprehensive and engaging overview of the broad themes in history that ran through the twentieth century.

John K. Jessup, ed., *The Ideas of Henry Luce.* New York: Atheneum, 1969. A representative selection of the writings of legendary journalist Henry R. Luce.

Don Lawson, *The KGB: The True Story of Russia's Spy Network!* New York: Julian Messner, 1984. A compelling examination of several notorious spy incidents, including the Rosenberg atomic spy case.

Richard Ned Lebow and Janice Gross Stein, *We All Lost the Cold War.* Princeton, NJ:

Princeton University Press, 1994. Using the Cuban missile crisis and the 1973 Arab-Israeli War as case studies, the authors provocatively conclude that nuclear deterrence policies prolonged the Cold War.

Peter Lyon, *Eisenhower: Portrait of the Hero.* Boston: Little, Brown, 1974. A thorough biography of an American war hero and president.

Karal Ann Marling, *As Seen on TV: The Visual Culture of Everyday Life in the 1950s.* Cambridge, MA: Harvard University Press, 1994. A fascinating examination of the visual culture of the 1950s, a unique window on postwar American sensibilities.

Myron A. Marty, *Daily Life in the United States, 1960–1990: Decades of Discord.* Westport, CT: Greenwood, 1997. A kaleidoscopic view of some of the most turbulent decades in U.S. history.

Robert Meeropol and Michael Meeropol, *We Are Your Sons: The Legacy of Ethel and Julius Rosenberg.* Urbana: University of Illinois Press, 1986. A spirited defense of the Rosenbergs by their sons, with an intriguing reexamination of the evidence in the atomic spy case.

John Newhouse, *War and Peace in the Nuclear Age.* New York: Alfred A. Knopf, 1989. An insightful modern history that brings the Cold War alive.

William Proxmire, *Report from Wasteland: America's Military-Industrial Complex.* New York: Praeger, 1970. Longtime U.S. senator Proxmire reveals breathtaking cost overruns and waste in defense spending.

Sam Roberts, *The Brother: The Untold Story of Atomic Spy David Greenglass and How He Sent His Sister, Ethel Rosenberg, to the Electric Chair.* New York: Random House, 2001. Provides a fascinating account of the atomic espionage case, based on the first interviews ever given by David Greenglass.

Carl Sagan and Richard Turco, *A Path Where No Man Thought: Nuclear Winter and the End of the Arms Race.* New York: Random House, 1990. Offers a harrowing look at the environmental hazards of even a "small" nuclear war, focusing on the phenomenon called nuclear winter.

Walter Schneir and Miriam Schneir, *Invitation to an Inquest.* Garden City, NY: Doubleday, 1965. A thorough examination of the Rosenberg atomic spy case.

Ellen Schrecker, *Many Are the Crimes: McCarthyism in America.* Boston: Little, Brown, 1998. A multifaceted look at the phenomenon of McCarthyism.

John Sharnik, *Inside the Cold War: An Oral History.* New York: Arbor House, 1987. A fascinating history of the Cold War, based on the ABC News special "45/85," as told by government officials and ordinary citizens.

John Steinbeck, *Travels with Charley in Search of America.* New York: Bantam Books, 1977. An enjoyable and insightful narrative of a cross-country journey by one of the nation's leading writers.

Richard B. Stolley, ed., *Life: Our Century in Pictures*. Boston: Bullfinch, 1999. A richly illustrated overview of the twentieth century.

Sam Tanenhaus, *Whittaker Chambers: A Biography*. New York: Random House, 1997. A fascinating biography of the former Communist spy whose allegations led to the downfall and imprisonment of a once highly respected State Department official.

Ralph de Toledano, *The Greatest Plot in History*. New Rochelle, NY: Arlington House, 1977. An engaging look at the Soviet Union's successful effort to steal atomic secrets from the United States.

Spencer R. Weart, *Nuclear Fear: A History of Images*. Cambridge, MA: Harvard University Press, 1988. A penetrating examination of the nuclear age and the fears that colored it.

Tim Weiner, *Blank Check: The Pentagon's Black Budget*. New York: Warner Books, 1990. A Pulitzer Prize–winning journalist sheds light on the Pentagon's secret budget in an insightful examination of the tensions between the need for both secrecy and accountability in defense spending.

Allen Weinstein, *Perjury: The Hiss-Chambers Case*. New York: Alfred A. Knopf, 1978. A detailed and entertaining examination of the Hiss-Chambers case, in which a former Communist spy accused a respected former State Department official of being a Communist spy.

Allen Weinstein and Alexander Vassiliev, *The Haunted Wood: Soviet Espionage in America, the Stalin Era*. New York: Random House, 1999. A thorough and thoughtful look at Soviet espionage in the United States, based on previously secret Soviet records.

Burke Wilkinson, ed., *Cry Spy! True Stories of 20th Century Spies and Spy Catchers*. Englewood Cliffs, NJ: Bradbury, 1969. A broad and interesting survey of celebrated spy cases, including selections on such Soviet spies as Julius and Ethel Rosenberg.

Allan M. Winkler, *The Cold War: A History in Documents*. Oxford: Oxford University Press, 2000. A fascinating and insightful look at the Cold War through photographs, speeches, government documents, political cartoons, and posters.

Elder Witt, ed., *Congressional Quarterly's Guide to the U.S. Supreme Court*. Washington, DC: Congressional Quarterly, 1979. A comprehensive history of the Supreme Court, its important rulings, and the justices who have served there.

Writers and Editors of The Associated Press, *Footprints on the Moon*. New York: Associated Press, 1969. A thrilling look at the U.S. space program, culminating in the historic moon landing and safe return of the astronauts of *Apollo 11*.

☆ Index ☆

★ Picture Credits ★

Cover Photo: © Bettmann/CORBIS
Associated Press, 41, 44, 47
© Bettmann/CORBIS, 24, 31, 32, 39, 49, 51, 56, 70, 75, 81, 85
© CORBIS, 7, 9, 10, 14
Hulton/Archive by Getty Images, 13, 15, 19, 20, 23, 26, 28, 29, 33, 37, 42, 57, 72, 78, 90
Minnesota Historical Society, 27
NASA, 54, 60, 63, 64, 66, 67
National Archives, 88
Ronald Reagan Library, 91
Steve Zmina, 11, 17, 83

★ About the Author ★

Geoffrey A. Campbell is a freelance writer in Fort Worth, Texas, where he is happily married to Linda, enjoys the rigors of being father to Mackenzie and Kirby, and is servant to two Persian cats. The St. Louis native is a graduate of the University of Missouri, where he earned a journalism degree. Geoff's work commonly appears in the *Fort Worth Star-Telegram*, for which he writes book reviews and occasional opinion pieces, and the *World Book Yearbook*, for which he writes articles relating to the U.S. government. He is a certified religious education teacher, a frequent school volunteer, and a youth sports coach. He enjoys working out regularly and plays hardball in both the Fort Worth Men's Senior Baseball League and the Dallas–Fort Worth National Adult Baseball Association. Previous titles include *The Pentagon Papers: National Security Versus the Public's Right to Know, The Persian Gulf War: Life of an American Soldier,* and *Thailand.*